Lucy Catlin Bull Robinson

A Child's Poems from October to October

1870-1871

Lucy Catlin Bull Robinson

A Child's Poems from October to October
1870-1871

ISBN/EAN: 9783744710558

Printed in Europe, USA, Canada, Australia, Japan

Cover: Foto ©Thomas Meinert / pixelio.de

More available books at **www.hansebooks.com**

A Child's Poems

From October to October,

1870-1871.

BY

LUCY CATLIN BULL,

(BORN APRIL 18, 1861.)

HARTFORD, CONN.

"But Mary kept all these things, and pondered them in her heart."

HARTFORD:

CASE, LOCKWOOD & BRAINARD.

1872.

NOTE FROM MR. WILLIAM C. BRYANT.

NEW YORK, Oct. 6, 1871.

I have looked over the poems of Lucy C. Bull, of Hartford, shown to me in manuscript. They seem to me most extraordinary for one so young, that is to say, of nine or ten years of age. They show a prodigious command of language considering her time of life, great ease of construction, an accurate ear for poetic numbers, and facility in the use of imagery not copied from books, but derived immediately from nature. I do not think I have seen any thing produced at the same age at all comparable to them.

WILLIAM CULLEN BRYANT.

626061

PREFACE.

It is thought best to print this private edition of a child's first poems for two reasons. First, to save the labor of supplying the large number of manuscript copies desired by friends; and secondly, to collect the poems themselves in a secure and more permanent form.

In doing this it is most earnestly desired that no more publicity may be given to the verses and their author than must necessarily accompany a book *privately printed.*

The arrangement of the book is simply in the order of the composition ; the object being to give a year's history of the working of the child's mind, as shown by her writings, rather than a volume of perfect poetry. For this reason, and for other obvious ones, no suggestions, corrections, or alterations have been made in any case. From title to end every poem is wholly original, and, with but few exceptions, they were withheld from parents and friends until completed.

As the little book will meet the eyes of many who do not know the author, it may be proper to say a few words with regard to her.

1*

From early childhood she has been keenly alive to impressions of grace and beauty, and her writing is a natural out- ·
pouring rather than a mental labor. Her health, so far from deteriorating, has steadily improved since this gift was developed. She has a strong and healthy inclination to all childish and even boisterous sports; great delight in the companionship of little children; and an even temperament, not subject to great exaltations or depressions. In a word, she is neither morbid nor precocious.

Fearing injury to her health, great care has been taken to avoid suggestion or pressure in the matter of her writing and reading; careful guiding of the latter being the only course adopted, and a holding back in study, writing and reading, so far as it could be done without arousing opposition and producing unhappiness: it being evidently the wiser course to surround her with pleasures and occupations that unconsciously to herself would in great measure take the place of mental work.

The "guiding of her reading" has consisted chiefly in withholding those books which in style or matter might have an injurious influence. Her own choice led her to make constant companions of Shakspeare and Milton, Scott's poems, and the Pilgrim's Progress, at so early an age as to surprise her parents. Later she became fond of Wordsworth, Tennyson and Bryant, and of her own accord took up Spenser's Faerie Queen with great delight.

At the age of nine years and a half she began her first regu-
lar attendance at school, a private seminary holding only a
morning session. She had long been in the habit of writing or
dictating little stories in prose, but at this time she remarked
to her mother, "I am going to write some poetry." "The
Wildwood" was the result of this first attempt, and was immediately re-written, and no one was permitted to see it until
some three months afterwards, when "The Country School-
House" and "Santa Claus' Visit" had been written; the
pleasure which these pieces gave her parents making her wil-
ling to show them her first effort.

From this beginning she wrote almost daily, often having
several pieces in her mind at once, but never being allowed to
write after dark. In reply to expressions of anxiety lest so
much writing should injure her health, she exclaimed, "They
come to me, I *must* write them; it is very easy, any one could
do it if they would only think so." "Toots's Lament" was in-
spired by hearing only that portion of Dombey and Son read
aloud; but both renderings were very unsatisfactory to herself.
The lines "On the Birthday of a Little Child" were found by
the servant hidden away under an oilcloth. Sorrow for the
loss of her life-long companion, produced the lines to Fido. A
friend visiting her mother, and drawing the contrast between
her two nieces, unconsciously suggested "Mabel's Good Be-
havior."

One Sunday, being prevented attending church, she said to
her mother, "I do not mean to write poetry on Sunday, but I
have a piece in my head, and I cannot rest until it is out; do
you think it would be wrong for me to write it down?" This
single exception to her rule was "The Wooing of Young Jockington." The next afternoon she went out with her sled, but
soon came in saying, 'she had so many pieces in her mind she
could not stay out, but it was so late she must choose the shortest
and easiest.' The "Ode to the Snowflake," and "Poetry
Everywhere" were the result of this choice. Her grandfather's
gift of a pair of canaries occasioned the lines dated February 3.
She said that "The Resurrection Hymn was composed while
swinging on a clothes line!" "The Poet's Dream" could not
be finished 'because she had not read the whole of Shakspeare.'
"Beautiful Rain" was written on the piazza during a shower;
"The Brook" and "The Baby's Breath," on the margin of a
newspaper while traveling in the cars; "An Evening Land-
scape," while alone in the upper chamber of a barn nestled in
the hay, the wide doors thrown open to the west. "Yanna"
and the Dramas were interspersed at intervals between the sixty
shorter poems.

J. P. B.

April, 1872.

CONTENTS.

vi CONTENTS.

Page.

CONTENTS.

𝔇ramas.

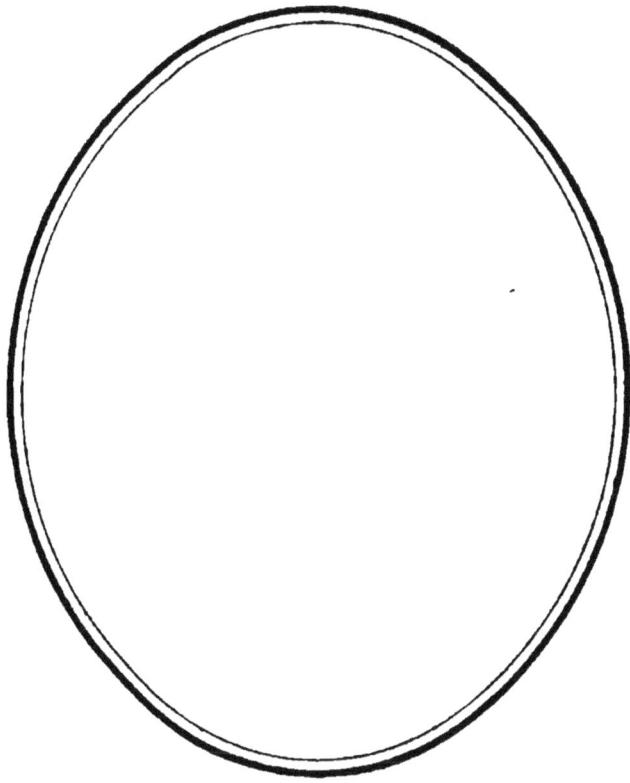

The Wildwood.

October, 1870.

I KNOW a spot where the violet grows,
And a mountain-brook through the forest flows
Down to the sea that murmurs low,
And dashes the foam as white as snow
Around the rocks, and o'er the sands,
And plays by the isle where the light-house stands.

'Tis beautiful there at the close of day,
When the painted butterfly ceases its play
To rest in calm and sweet repose,
On the soft warm heart of the sweet red rose.
Then the daisy shuts its golden eye,
And the insects cease their hum and fly.

I love to roam at dawn of day,
And list to the wild birds' morning lay ;
Then all the flowers are waking up,
And the water-lily opes its cup,
The sun sends down its warming rays,
And the little brook with the pebbles still plays.

2

The Wildwood.

As First Written.

I KNOW a spot where the wild thyme blows,
Where the wind caresses the sweet red rose,
Where human foot doth seldom tread
On the soft green moss that makes a bed
  For the modest violet.

I love to roam at dawn of day
In its realms where the beautiful butterflies play,
For there is peace and joyfulness
E'en to the blades of soft green grass
  That peep up from the moss.

The Country School-House.

December 17, 1870.

IT stands upon a grassy plain,
  Amid the elm-trees tall,
That stretch their branches far in vain
  To catch the stars so small.

But hark! the school-bells ring
  For nine o'clock at morn,
See the children coming in
  With book under each arm.

With many a shout and merry din
  They pour in at the door,
Their lunches in their pails of tin,
  Oh, me! just hear them roar!

The old schoolmaster he is there,
  So dignified and tall,
With stature large and figure spare,
  He seems to fill the hall.

He taps the desk and school begins.
    The children take their seats ;
They laugh and whisper, play with pins,
    And many other feats.

At last the bell rings—school is done—
    How glad the children are !
With many a joke and many a pun,
    They run out in the air.

And now they're gone, the school-room's bare
    And still and empty as the night,
Except a straggler here and there,
    That stayed to fly his kite.

Santa-Claus' Visit.

December 20, 1870.

,'TWAS a merry Christmas eve,
  The snow was falling fast ;
The time when folks believe
  Old Santa-Claus comes past.
The children hung their stockings
  At the chimney-corner tall—
Even little Toddlekins
  Hung up her stocking small.

But hark ! what means this knocking
  In the chimney, who is that?
'Tis Santa-Claus that's coming,
  I thought it was a rat.
Look, look ! his head is peeping—
  How funny he does seem !
He looks to see 'f they're sleeping
  So that he can't be seen.

2*

Now see ! he's coming out,—
    Oh me ! how he does act !
How carefully he moves about
    So he shan't drop his pack !
Here is a doll for Chris—
    And, oh dear me ! what's that ?
A rocking-horse for Bob,
    And next a squeaking cat.

And here's a drum for Tom,
    A little trumpet next,
Then a dollie that came from
    Paris, in rose-silk dressed ;
And then for Toddlekins a doll
    To ope and shut its eye ;
And then a parrot, pretty Poll !
    And a baby that can cry.

And now his work is done,
    The stockings all are filled—
Not even a sugar-plum
    Upon the floor he's spilled.

And now he's gone, the children sleep
   And dream sweet dreams all night,
Till the morn begins to peep
   And the sun shines bright.

Mr. Toots's Lament for Florence.

January 11, 1871.

FLORENCE, my own true love!
   Listen to me my dove—
Your dangers all with love I'd fence,
But still it is no consequence.

I never expected nor dreamed that
Burgess and Co. would make this hat
With band around, to show the love
I feel for you, my cooing dove.

And now I'll end this sad romance—
'Tis not the slightest consequence;
Accept, I beg you, this nonsense,
O'er which so many hours I've spent.

Mr. Toots's Lament—No. 2.

January, 1871.

DEAR Florence, if I might hope,
    Though 'tis no consequence;
You know if I might hope
    I'd stand in your defence.

I walk the streets in sheer despair,
    I'd die for love of thee;
Despair! despair goes through my hair
    When betrothed pairs I see.

And now I'll end this sad romance,
    My devoted love you see;
A broken-hearted man I am
    Despairing for love of thee.

On the Birth-Day of a Little Child.

January, 1871.

THOU art one year old, my darling child,—
  Twelve months have passed since first I held thee in
    my arm ;
Sweet, gentle, trusting, meek, and mild,
  One year thy God hath kept thee from all harm.

Thou art one year old—yes, one year old,
  And still thou art more dear to me
Than all the merchants' shining gold
  That comes across the sea.

I pray to God to keep
  Thee safe another year ;
May angels watch thy sleep,
  Then thou canst never fear.

Charade.—Fido.

January, 1871.

  My first is in fie, but not in shame,
  My second is in dough, but not in bread,
  My whole is the name of an animal.

On the Death of a Favorite Dog.

FIDO died Jan. 24, 1871, aged eleven years.

'TIS only a little dog, and yet
   It spreads a gloom upon the place,—
No one can ever him forget,
   No one can ever him replace.

No more he'll meet me at two o'clock,
   No more he'll bark at the horses shy,—
Oh Fido! such a dreadful shock!
   So cold and stiff you there do lie.

'Twas but yesternight, yesternight!
   It seems as if it could not be;
Art in the snow so cold and white?
   Oh Fido! look once more to me!

No more you'll go to the market with me,
   No more for strawberries red and round;
I weep when your little grave I see,
   To think of you in the cold, cold ground.

The Wooing of Young Jockington.

A Scottish Ballad.

Jan. 29, 1871.

NOW gather round the fire,
   Ye warriors brave and true,
And the wooing of young Jockington
   I will relate to you.

In Scotland fair there lived a maid,
   Fair to the eye was she,
With rosy cheeks and hazel eyes,
   The lily of the lea.

Now there lived a lad, young Jockington,
   Who tended flocks of sheep,
Who fell in love with Jennie fair,
   Oft causing him to weep.

One day while he was tending sheep
   He saw the lassie fair,
Come running o'er the mountain,
   Through the violets rare.

In her hand she held a pitcher
　　Filled with water clear,
Just returning from the fountain
　　He saw as she came near.

" How do you do, young Jennie ?"
　　And " how do you do, young James ?"
" Now stay awhile young Jennie,
　　To watch the lambkins' games."

" Oh no, I cannot stay," quoth she,
　　" For grandam waits at home;"
" But never mind your grandam, lass,
　　Come, lass, and with me roam."

So, partly from his teasing
　　She stayed with the young lad ;
The emerald fields were waving,
　　And the nightingale sang sad.

When the murmur of sweet waters
　　Came from the river Dee,
The lassie stopped and listened—
　　" 'Tis my grandam calling me !"
　3

" Oh, no," said James, " 'tis the river,
   'Tis the azure river Dee,
That floweth on forever,
   And softly sings to me."

*   *   *   *   *   *   *

I cannot tell you, warriors,
   How it all came about,
But 'tis certain they were married
   Two weeks after their rout.

Ode to a Snow-Flake.

January 30, 1871.

PURE as crystal, light as feather,
  Flying through the chilly air,
Pausing at some bunch of heather,
  Clear and dazzling, white and fair.

Tell me, tell me, little snow-flake
  What do you, on this great earth?
You're so small no one can need you,
  You are dancing now with mirth.

" Gentle, cheerful little maiden,
  I come down from the great sky ;
I come down with all my brothers,
  I come from the clouds so high.

We are covering up the meadows
  Where you used to run and play ;
One by one we're softly falling
  Through the chilly winter's day."

Mabel's Good Behavior.

January 29, 1871.

ORDERLY Mabel, at the table
  Always behaved as she ought;
Neat, precise, and very sable,*
  Always acted as she'd been taught.

Orderly, careful, was this maiden,
  Different from her sister Lou;
Her heart with duties overladen—
  She was politer than a Jew.

Very neat was her hand-writing;
  She could write as well as Lou—
Never quarreling, never fighting,
  Mabel is the pattern for you.

---

*The author explains that when this was written she thought *sable* meant *sober*
Also that this piece was not intended for poetry, but merely for rhyme.

Poetry Everywhere.

January 30, 1871.

POETRY, poetry everywhere!
  You breathe it in the summer air,
You see it in the green wild woods,
It nestles in the first spring buds.

You find it in the primrose rare,
'Tis in the apple blossom fair,
It smiles in maidens and in youths,
You taste it in the apple-juice!

'Tis poetry, poetry, everywhere—
It nestles in the violets fair,
It peeps out in the first spring grass—
Things without poetry are very scarce!

3*

The Forget-me-not: A Tale of Germany.

February 2, 1871.

FAR, far in distant Germany
   There dwelt a peasant poor,
Who had no children save Janet,
   A maiden fair and pure.

Stern poverty did often break
   Upon that little cot,
But still the little family lived
   Contented with their lot.

Now Jennie's love was " honest John,"
   A goodly man was he,.
Known round the country by that name
   For his great honesty.

But soon he'd leave fair Germany
   For countries far away,
Till he'd come back both rich and great,
   And they'd be married gay.

Two days before he left her,
  A lovely day was that,
They strolled the woods together,
  And by the brookside sat;

And creeping all around it
  Grew the forget-me not;
Growing down to the water's edge,
  Their flowers just a dot.

Then Johnnie plucked the fairest
  And gave it to Janet,
Saying, " Oh, forget-me-not,
  And I'll come back, my pet!"

The pearly tears stood in her eyes,
  She took the little flower,
Saying. "Oh Johnnie, I'll be true to you,
  And love you with all my power."

Two days had cast their shadows down
  Upon the wide, wide earth,
When Johnnie sailed for England
  Out of the little firth.

A year had passed since Johnnie sailed
  Away from Germany;
A year of watching and suspense
  To the maid of Hanover,—

When, one day while she was sitting
  As she often used to do,
Thinking of her dear Johnnie,
  And the forget-me-not blue,

The door wide opened, she sprang up—
  She knew 'twas her dear John;
Then in his arms he folded her
  Regardless of her gown.

The next day they were married
  In pomp and splendor gay,
And lived together happily
  For many a goodly day.

Our Canaries.

February 3, 1871.

HANGING up in the ceiling,
  Billing and cooing all day,
Are our darling Canary birds,
  As happy as if it were May.

In the long winter evenings
  When it is dark and cold,
Dickie beguiles us with singing,
  I would not sell them for gold.

Hopping, hopping, hopping,
  On the long wooden pegs,
With yellow backs and saucy black eyes,
  And funny little pink legs.

They are the dearest little things,
  And the sunshine of my heart,
With little bills and funny wings,
  I never with them will part.

The Old Lamplighter.

February 3, 1871.

SLOWLY, slowly, one by one,
  The old lamplighter goes
Lighting each lamp in its turn,
  Till they sparkle gay in rows.

His coat is ragged, his hair is gray,
  His face is thin and wan ;
He has lighted lamps for many a day
  In the noisy, busy town.

Each day he grows thinner, each day he grows old,
  Yet each day he lights the lamps ;
Be the weather warm, or be it cold,
  Still he goes on his nightly tramps.

His house is a poor one, his money is scarce,
  And nobody cares for old Joe,
But still he goes on, each night lighting the gas,
  And each evening he makes it glow.

Music.

February 3, 1871.

SOFTLY, softly o'er me stealing,
  Comes sweet music soft and low ;
O'er the meadows softly breathing,
  O'er the newly fallen snow.

By the brooklet softly sighing,
  I love to lie and list to it
Far off in the blue hills dying ;
  There do I most love to sit.

Charade.—Poetry.

MY first is in Poland, but not in Spain,
  My second is in get, but not in gain ;
My third is in merry, but not in glee,
My whole is in everything that I see.

Evening Lullaby.

February 4, 1871.

LULLABABY, lullababy!
Angels watch you while you sleep,
When the stars begin to peep,
Pleasant dreams around you play
While you sleep the time away;
Naughty dreams, go! take your flight
From my baby-girl to-night—
>> Hushaby!

Lullababy, lullababy!
Now your eyes are closing fast,
My baby-girl's asleep at last;
Bye, bye, darling, mama's here, .
Don't you see her? she's quite near.
Now the moon is brightly shining
On her couch of stars reclining—
>> Hushaby!

Lullababy, lullababy!
Sleep, and dream sweet dreams all night,
Sleep until the sun shines bright;
Then my baby'll ope her eyes,
And up with the lark she'll rise;
Then when he is singing gay
You will get up, my little May—
Hushaby!

Valentine.—To Bessie.

February 13, 1871.

MY dear cousin Bessie, I wish you good health,
  And a pleasant St. Valentine's day,
With valentines plenty to add to your wealth,
  And beguile all your pretty play.

4

The Violets.

February 17, 1871.

DOWN beneath the hedges,
  Growing in the grass,
Violets are my favorites,
  I loved them when a lass.

Growing in the meadows,
  Growing in the fields,
Everywhere the violet
  Its little blossom yields.

In the stately garden
  Is the handsome rose,
While the little violet
  'Neath the hedges grows.

Gentle little violet,
  Never knows a care,
Free from pain and sorrow,
  Modest, sweet and fair.

Evening at the Old Homestead.

February, 1871.

THE evening shades are flitting,
  And the tallow-lamp shines bright;
Grandmama sits a-knitting
  By the crimson firelight.

Grandpa sits with snowy hair,
  Dreaming of years long past,
In front of the fire's reddening glare,
  With the light on his features cast.

Faithful old Fido lies at their feet,
  Sleeping away the day;
Tabby is purring softly and sweet,
  While her kitten is at play.

And many years will come before
  This picture be removed;
When Tabby'll be too old to claw
  The mice she once had loved.

Under the Coverlid; or the Morning Frolic.

February 27, 1871.

UNDER the coverlid dotted with green,
  Two little rosy cheeks may be seen ;
Two little eyes are winking with fun,
Can't keep themselves open before the great sun ;
Two cherry lips so merry and sweet,
Two little hands and two little feet.

Now Bessie darling, she must arise,
Then she must open those little blue eyes;
But Bessie is roguish and mischievous too,
And though she will open those eyes of blue,
She's dancing o'er coverlid and o'er sheet
In her long nightie and little bare feet.

But see ! mama's caught her and folded her tight.
Away from the sun's glaring reddening light ;
And now Bessie's going down stairs to sup
Some nice bread and milk from her little red cup ;
For mama has dressed her and brushed her soft hair,
And washed her round face with sweet loving care.

The Geranium.

February 27, 1871.

I ROAMED throughout the garden,
 I roamed throughout the field,
And every little blossom
 Its sweet perfume did yield.
The lily and the rose were there,
And the gentle little maiden-hair.

But something still was wanting,
 Though I could not tell what ;
The air was filled with fragrance
 From every yard and lot.
I saw the pink and violet,
The heliotrope and mignonette.

But suddenly I smelt a breath
 So sweet and pure and clear,
I knew 'twas the geranium
 The moment I came near.
I handled it, and oh ! so sweet it smelt !
I plucked a leaf and put it in my belt.
 4*

The Rainbow.

February 27, 1871.

RISING in the lofty mountain,
  Stretching through the atmosphere,
Gleaming in some playful fountain,
  Off so far, and yet so near.

Bow of promise ! far extending
  Through the misty, rainy land,
In the low green valley bending,
  All a colored, shining band.

The Firelight; or Childhood's Memories.

February 27, 1871.

I Love to sit by the firelight,
   When the stars peep out, and the moon shines bright,
And think of my childhood's happy days,
And of all my pleasures and all my plays.

I used to play 'neath the apple-tree,
And there with my dollies I'd take real tea;
Then I and my darling sister Bess,
We'd go to the pantry and make a mess.

We played at milkmaid, we played at horse,
And then to each other a ball we'd toss;
We swung in the swing, we sat in the teenter.
We jumped off the roof of the house—'twas a lean-to!

And I'll never forget childhood's happy day,
Though my hand grow withered, and my hair grow gray,
And I love to sit and build castle-towers,
And think myself again in those hours.

To Grandpa on his Birth-Day.

With a copy of her Verses.

February 28, 1871.

DARLING old grandpa with silvery hair,
  Thy birth-day has come by;
Funny old grandpa is growing old,
  The short years swiftly fly.

Darling old grandpa with silvery hair,
  Accept this little book,
O'er which I've labored with much care,
  And filled up every nook.

To the Lily of the Valley.

March 1, 1871.

LITTLE flower of spotless white,
  Hiding 'neath the sun's red light,
Pointed are thy leaves of green,
'Neath spring grasses thou art seen.

Give me not the rose so proud,
Nor the candytuft with shroud,
Nor the blue forget-me-nots,
Nor the pinks, for there are lots.

Give me not the mignonette,
Nor the modest violet ;
But the lily of the vale is mine,
With silver bells and emerald shrine.

Little flower, pure and sweet,
Softly hiding at my feet,
Other flowers ne'er'll surpass
Gentle lily's spotless face.

The Tale of the Bee.

March 7, 1871.

A VIOLET sweetly reposing one day—
A sunshiny time in the month of May,
Was startled to hear a buzzing sound
From close beside her, above the green ground;
'Twas the busy bee, and she heard him say,
" Madam, your honey I want to-day."

" I pray you," the violet sweetly did say,
" Why do you come here every day
For honey, and yet never stop to take
One little drop, e'en for hunger's sake ?
This I would very much like to know
If you will tell me before you go."

" Yes, Madam," replied the courteous bee,
" As soon as I've just run up this tree
And got more honey, I will return
And then, sweet creature, you shall learn
What the reason is that such as I,
Backward and forward busily fly."

Thus with many thanks from the violet blue,
The bee flew away to his labor true;
But soon he returned softly buzzing away,
And this is what he to the violet did say.
I'll tell it the same as 'twas told to me
By a robin up in the apple tree.

" We live in a hive with holes for our doors,
And plenty of honey laid up on our floors,
So when winter comes round we do nothing but eat,
Or sleep through the days in slumbers sweet;
Our queen is just and gracious too,
She says she has seen the violet blue,

And privately thinks of all pretty flowers
She ne'er saw a sweeter in all her hours.
But I must be off, do not ask me to stay."
So saying the courteous bee flew away;
But often the violet thought of that day,
And of all the honey-bee had to say.

The Anemone.

March 9, 1871.

'NEATH the greenwood trees and the forest elms,
In the secret places of forest realms,
There lieth a flower of delicate pink.
So sweet 'twere from fairy-land you would think ;
'Tis anemone with her delicate robe
Of soft wildwood mosses for her lovely green globe.

Modest and meek 'neath the greenwood tree,
Little anemone you may see ;
Dear little anemone, forest-child,
Gentle and delicate, sweet and mild ;
In your May-day forest and meadow-tour
You see sweet anemone fair and pure.

To Bessie LeB. Fletcher.

March 1, 1871.

JUMPING in her mama's arms,
Free from cares and free from harms,
    Little Bessie !

Little arms so plump and round,
In her little dressing-gown,
    Is my Bessie !

Papa's darling, mama's pride,
Bessie come and take a ride
    On her papa's knee !

Little eyes and soft brown hair,
Bessie is a baby rare,
    Cunning Bessie !

You may search each house in town,
There's no baby all around
    Like my Bessie !

5

Ode to the Violet.

March 9, 1871.

THE rose may spread her mantle fine
 Of petals pink, and leafy shrine,
The lily too may shake her bells,
The ferns may grow about the wells,
  ·But they are not for me.

'Tis not the little maiden-hair,
'Tis not the heartsease sweet and fair,
Nor the forget-me-not so blue,
No, none of these to me are true,
  Not one of these for me.

Little flower of azure blue,
Violet to me is true,
Hiding oft her modest head
'Neath her leafy, mossy bed,—
  Violets for me.

The Three Mothers; or the Patters of Little Feet.

March 13, 1871.

THREE women sat in the parlor neat,
And listed to patters of little feet;
Then each one spake of her pride and dear,
And they crept together closer and near.

The first one spake with a joyous face,
" There ne'er was such beauty, there ne'er was such grace,
As are seen in our darling little Annette,
The family pride and the family pet.

" Her eyes are of the Spaniard dark,
Her hair the color of the lark,
With merry lips and rosy cheeks,
And soft eye lashes 'gainst soft eye-peeps."

The second spake with beaming eyes,
" There ne'er was a darling of such small size
As our little Tot, 'bout as big as a mouse,
We could put her into the baby-house.

" She has sweet blue eyes and auburn curls,
To me she's the prettiest of all little girls ;
With her pretty, graceful, winning way,
And smile as bright as the dawn of day."

Then the third one heaved a heavy sigh.
And raised her eyes to heaven on high—
" My children up in heaven are gone,
And I am left childless and alone !

" The first one filled my heart with joy,
It was a darling little boy,
And while he lived so calm and pure,
The thought of his dying I could not endure.

" But he died !   Then came two little girls,
With soft brown eyes and soft brown curls ;
But now they up in heaven are gone,
And 'tis empty and dreary now at home.

" And they sound to me like music sweet,
When I list to patters of little feet."
And many a pitying tear dropped there,
They thought she was a mother rare.

May.

March 18, 1871.

'TIS beautiful in the month of May,
 When the robins are billing and singing all day ;
Then the blue birds build in the old street elms,
And the squirrel leaps in the forest realms,
And the children watch for the maple buds,
And anemones blossom in fields and woods.
Then the blossoms bloom on the apple tree,
And dandelions flourish by hill and lea,
And the brooklets babble in the grass-green vale,
And the lambkins play by hill and dale ;
And I love to roam in the month of May,
When everything's happy and everything's gay.

5*

The Soldiers' Parting.

(Suggested by an incident related in a Sermon by Rev. N. J. Burton,
D. D., Park Church, Hartford.)

March 20, 1871.

I WANDERED in the little street
  Where all was hushed and still;
No patters from the horses' feet,
  No music from the rill.

Two young men stood in soldiers' blue,
  One held a little child,
And looked into her eyes so true,
  With such expression mild.

And here the *wife* stood weeping by,
  'Twas a sad sight to see,
Her husband in the war would die
  Upon the battle lea.

And on the porch the *mother* stood,
  Shading her eyes so blue,
Her boys would sacrifice their blood
  To their dear country true.

But worst of all, so sad and true,
   The *father* stood so brave,
And gazed upon those coats of blue—
   Thought of them in a grave.

And never, never, I'll forget
   The influence of that day,
I thought of all the other world,
   So thoughtless and so gay.

Ode to a Sunset.

March 20, 1871.

FAST sinking 'neath thy rosy skies, oh sun!
  Fast sinking ere the weary day be done,
Thou bringest thought of days of happy yore,
Those happy days shall bloom for us no more.
Thou tell'st me of those days of infancy,
Which, wondering, stops its play to gaze on thee,
Thy rosy bloom and azure cloudy sky.
But farewell, sun! farewell those happy days of yore!
Farewell! I see thee now no more, no more!

Ode to Venus.

March 21, 1871.

STAR of the evening! belle of the night!
Shining with lustre sparkling and bright!
Lightly ascend to thy beautiful throne,
Lightly put on thy bright evening crown!

Each star adores thee, shines at the oft,
Now let the moon sing thy lullaby soft;
Rocking in heavens, shining so bright,
Sparkling with lustre, shedding thy light.

Now farewell to Venus, beautiful star!
Lightly ascend to thy swift cloudy car;
Star of the heavens, shining above,
Emblem of peace and emblem of love!

What Is It?

March 27, 1871.

WHAT mean these eyes so bright and black ?
What this embroidered little sacque ?
What mean these rosy cheeks so fair and round ?
What this little green dressing gown ?
And these little arms so chubby and fat?
These locks of hair soft as our furry cat?
These two little lips so merry and sweet ?
These tiny arms and these kicking feet?
And this little ear as red as a rose,
And this double chin and this little nose ?
I fear I must tell you or you'll never guess,
'Tis our little darling baby Bess !

Hast Ever?

March 30, 1871.

TELL me, tell me! old brown rock,
Hast ever caught a fairy lock?
Say, hast thou sheltered a wandering fay,
In April showers or at close of day?
Tell me, knotted oak so old,
Hast ever hidden fairy gold?
Tell me, gentle sloping hill,
Tell me, little babbling rill,
Have fairies ever danced on thee?
I'm sure fays' footsteps I can see!
Tell me, oh! tell me this I pray,
Tell me, hast ever seen a fay?

Address to a Nightingale.

April, 1871.

SWEET bird that mournest in the forest deep,
  That spreadst thy mantle of dark simple gray,
Thou art the poet's company and life;
Thou bird that sing'st so mournfully thy lay,
The poet doth rejoice in thee sweet one!
Thou art his thought, his heart, his joy, his son.
He puts aside his lab'rous work and lists
To thee, sweet bird, fair winning nightingale!
That mournest, singest in the lonely dale,
With but the poet for thy company,
But now adieu, sweet bird, farewell, farewell!

The Child and the Cloud.

April 3, 1871.

CHILD.

LITTLE cloud far up so high,
 Floating in the azure sky,
Tell me what use art thou to earth,
Thou playful creature full of mirth;
For often I have heard it said
All things for some good use are made.

CLOUD.

Little maiden, mild and meek,
What I'm good for would'st thou seek?
Once was I part of the sea,
People used to sail on me,
But bye and bye I rose up high,
And now am floating in the sky.
But I'll not always stay up there,
Floating in the balmy air,
Bye and bye I'll form in rain,

6

Come down to the earth again,
Water all the little plants
In wood and gardens' secret haunts.
If 'tis winter then I'll freeze,
Drop down on the apple trees ;
This my use is, little maid,
That's the reason I was made.

A Vision of the Future.

April 7, 1871.

I SAT within my study lost in thought,
   'Twas then I slept and dreamed this lovely dream.
  I dreamt the future was before me brought,
I saw the scenes I'd passed through in life's team ;
  I saw myself a soldier brave and free,
Fighting and struggling fiercely hand to hand.
  Next, father, with three children at my knee,
And husband, too, with sweetest wife so bland.
  And then a widower, bowed by age and care,
And then a cripple limping with much pain ;
  No longer beauty'd smile on me so fair
As once he did, or youth in every vein.
  And then I woke and found I had but slept,
  But since that time forever have I kept
  That dream all safely locked up in my heart,
  And with it never, never will I part.

Childhood's Memories.

April, 1871.

THERE are many things that cluster
  Round childhood's happy dreams,
But my gentle, loving parents
  Are the sweetest now it seems.

I had a gentle mother
  Of never ceasing love,
And she told me of that Father
  Who looketh from above.

She read to me the Bible,
  God's sacred, holy book,
And of the blessed Jesus
  Who never us forsook.

She used to tell me stories
  As I sat upon her knee,
Of her childhood's happy hours,
  E'en now her face I see.

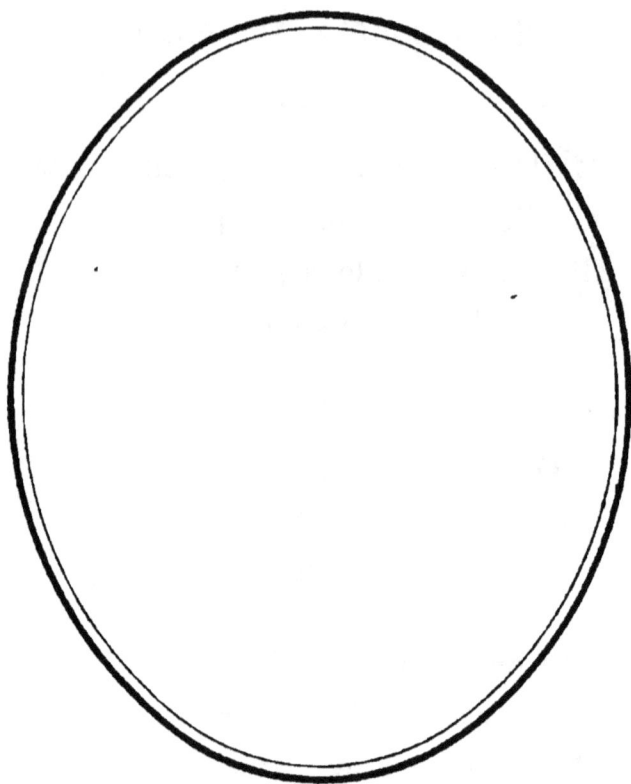

And then my darling father,
  Who Latin taught to me,
And hugged me closely to him
  As I sat upon his knee.

We often went blackberrying
  In the forest deep and dark,
And I oft would stand and listen
  To the singing of the lark.

And now they come around me,
  As I sit and think alone, ˙
Watching and waiting for me,
  Till I rise to that great Throne.

And never I'll forget them
  Unto my dying day,
My gentle, loving parents,
  Thoughts of you ne'er'll go away.

6*

To a Cluster of Violets.

April, 1871.

I WANDERED in the forest on the hill,
I roamed beside the brook that turns the mill,
I plucked the primrose and arbutus pink
Along its eddying, babbling, cooling brink.
I plucked forget-me-nots so meek and blue,
They too beside its grass-green margin grew ;
But as along the valley did I pass
I spied a cluster of blue violets in the grass.
Now, for the flowers I plucked before I did not care,
But threw them all on the green moss there,
And gathered violets till there were none,
And the bright emerald leaves were left alone.
Oh sweet they smelt ! so beautiful and fair !
And blue as skies, yet modesty was there,
Bending their necks beneath their leaves so green,
Till scarce a little flower could be seen.
Then I pressed them closer, closer to my lips.—
Since then I've been on many forest trips,
But never one that I enjoyed more
Than when beside the brooklet's babbling pour,
I gathered violets to my heart's content,
Sweet flowers ! with their heads so meekly bent.

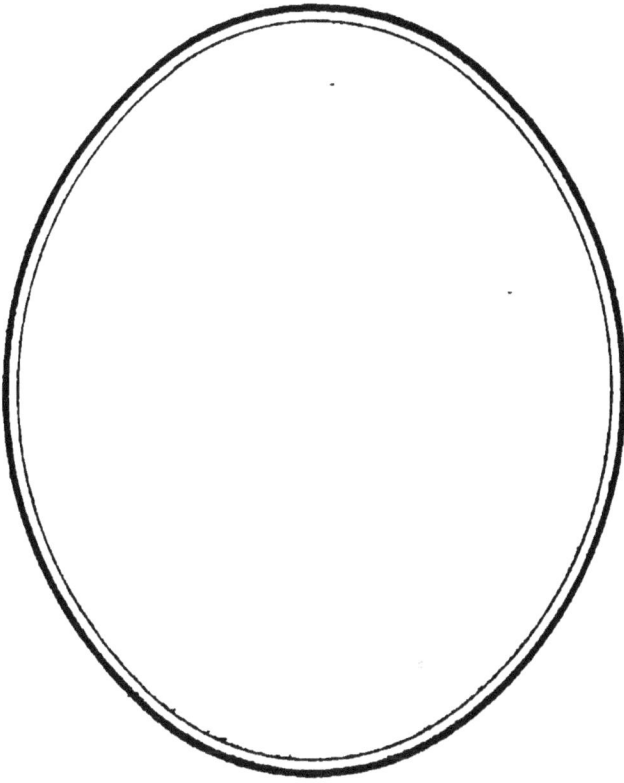

A Lament for Little Fido.

April 11, 1871.

WHEN I roam about the orchard,
  In the meadow, in the field,
I have no little Fido
  To be my careful shield.

The days are long and dreary,
  And I sit and think alone,
Why my darling little Fido
  Away from me is gone.

I have no heart for pleasure,
  I have no heart for play,
But I think of little Fido,
  And why he went away.

And even now I wonder
  Why I was left alone,
Why we were torn asunder
  And I left so forlorn.

The birds are singing blithely
  Up in the apple tree,
But I've no heart for music
  Now Fido's gone from me.

For all about that orchard
    We used to play and run,
With the violets beneath us,
    And above shone bright the sun.

And I see him now a-playing
    Beneath the apple trees,
With his merry bark a-straying
    Far on the summer breeze.

The violets are blooming
    Down in the fresh green grass,
And the brooklet soft is tuning
    Where Fido used to pass.

The children now are shouting,
    Just coming home from school,
But they only make me lonely,
    And my eyes with tears fill full.

Oh, my darling little Fido!
    Shall I no more see thee?
I e'en now hear the barking
    Upon the grassy lea.

Mandoline.

April 22, 1871.

SWEET Mandoline sitting beneath the trees,
  Letting thy wild song float on the breeze,
With fresh blooming roses thy brow is entwined,
And the flowers sweet perfumes send to thee on the wind.
Thy feet thou art bathing in the cool brooklet's flow,
Where sweet blue forget-me-nots clustering grow,—
Thy long Spanish hair thou hast taken down
So that it almost touches the ground.
Such is the dream that wins my heart,
With so sweet a picture ne'er can I part;
So haste thee, sweet Mandoline, haste to my side,
And I will make thee my winning bride.

A Hymn of the Resurrection.

Dedicated to my loving Parents.

May 21, 1871.

COME ye saints that do rejoice
  In the blessed Saviour's name,
Enter into heavenly joys,
  And His peaceful kingdom claim.
Far beyond the crystal river,
There is peace and joy forever.

There with golden harps you'll sing,
  There you'll wear a golden crown;
Forever let your praises ring
  For Christ the Lamb, the spotless One.
Far beyond the crystal river
Sing His praises loud forever.

In the kingdom of your Lord
  Rest, oh rest, ye weary saints!
'Neath His sheltering wings' abode,
  There the hungry soul ne'er faints.
Far beyond the crystal river
Rest within your Lord forever.

There the tree of life doth bloom,
  There 'tis day and never night,
For Christ, who drives away all gloom,
  Brighter doth shine than earthly light.
Far beyond the crystal river
He shines with blessed light forever.

Once He lived on earth for us,
  Healed the sick, poor, and insane;
Died upon the bloody cross,
  And rose to heaven again to reign.
Now beyond the crystal river
He reigns in peace and joy forever.

Then come ye saints that do rejoice
  In His blessed, holy Name,
Enter to His holy joys,
  And His peaceful kingdom claim.
Far beyond the crystal river
Dwell with Him in peace forever.

Only Six Years Old.

May 31, 1871.

ONLY a little maiden
  With curly hair of gold,
Only a red-cheeked darling,
  Only six years old.

Only a pearly forehead,
  Only sweet cherry lips two,
Only a little hand lily white,
  Only large eyes of blue.
  *   *   *   *   *
Only a stilled chamber,
  Only a form white and cold,
Only a sleeping infant,
  Only six years old.

Only a little angel
  Safe in the heavenly fold,
Only up with Jesus
  Walking those streets of gold.

Only two weeping parents,
  Only an empty room,
Awed and darkened and silent,
  Overhung with gloom.

The Poet's Dream.

(Unfinished.)

May, 1871.

'TIS evening, and the stars do peep,
  Bright 'shines the winter moon,
Old Shakspeare lieth fast asleep
  In the midst of evening's gloom.
Fast, fast asleep, and this great man
Dreams over what he wrote, again.

Titania gay, the fairy queen,
  Now doth her revels hold,
And Oberon, her king, is seen
  With all his fairy gold.
Bassanio now his love doth win,
A golden ring she giveth him.

Duke Frederick, with angry look,
  Fair Rosalind doth banish;
Here cometh Corin with a crook,
  Now Adam old doth famish.
Hermione again doth live,
  Doth to Perdita blessings give.

7

Verses Composed in a Hammock.

June 19, 1871.

OH! I love and I love to roam in the dell,
   Where the lily shaketh her crystal bell,
Where the birds twitter secrets above in the tree,
And the sweetest songs they sing to me;
And I sit in my hammock and swing and swing,
Happier far than many a king.

Beautiful Rain.

(Written on the piazza during a shower.)

June 28, 1871.

BEAUTIFUL, beautiful, beautiful rain!
    Making the brooklet dance in the glen,
Making the daisy lift up its head,
Filling with water the tulip-cups red,
Making the lawn grass fresh and green,
While in the distance a rainbow is seen.

Beautiful rain! so refreshing and cool!
Making us holidays out of school,
Making music of nature sweet and soft,
Pattering, knocking on the brown roof aloft,
Falling o'er forest and valley and plain,
Beautiful, beautiful, beautiful rain!

The Brook.

July 14, 1871.

RUSH along the lofty mountain's steep,
I murmur in the forest wild and deep,
Until I reach the azure sea at last,
And on her azure bosom safe am cast.

I overflow the orchards and the lots,
And water freely the forget-me-nots,
That nestle by my side confidingly
Beneath the gentle weeping willow tree.

I carol in the peaceful meadows green,
Where her purple mantle dons the violet fair ;
I roam in woods where blooms the eglantine,
Where wild primroses scent the balmy air.

And still I chatter, babble, laugh and carol,
And dash my spray upon the mountain laurel,
Then flee away, laughing, in full career,
As swift and fleet as any mountain deer.

The Baby's Breath.

July 14, 1871.

OH baby! where didst get thy breath, where?
  Did zephyrs bring it thee?
Did it float to thee from the blossom fair
  Of the scented orange tree?
Did some fairy wing it to thee so fleet?
Or art thou some new-born flower sweet?

Oh, say! whence cometh this golden hair?
  Whence these eyes of ocean blue?—
She raised them to mine with a sudden air,
  "I know! I got them from you!"

The Farmer's Baby.

July 19, 1871.

"I SHOULD like to know what's the use of a baby!
To make everybody trouble may be!
Allers a kickin' 'n squallin' 'n rollin',
A-doin' mischief 'n cryin' 'n foolin',
Fallin' bumpity-bump adown the stairs,
Gittin' knocked under tables 'n pinched under chairs,
Knockin' head agen doors 'n gittin' it bruised,
'N screechin' 'n thinkin' its bein' abused.
'N when I come in from hard work at my plough,
It's 'step softly! *don't* wake her! she's fast asleep now!'
They call her a 'precious,' 'n 'rosebud,' 'n 'pearl,'—
For my part I don't see much good in a *girl*,
And my head will soon be in a terrible whirl
If they don't send that squallin' young infant away,
THAT'S the one thing that baby *is* good for *I* say!"

Baby-Boy.

July 19, 1871.

WITH tiny pink hands and mouth shaped like a bow,
With pearly forehead as white as snow,
Baby-boy.

With a dimpled chin and tiny head,
Bald and round and smooth and red,
Baby-boy.

With blackberry eyes of a startling gaze,
Inquiringly looking up in your face,
Baby-boy.

Now Benny is going out for a ride,
"Wis booful flowers on every side,"
Holding his toy,
Good-bye, baby-boy!
I wish you joy!

The May Wreath.

July 26, 1871.

WITH what shall I crown thy brow fair queen?
　　With the blushing rose or the eglantine?
With the tall bright pinks so fair and sweet?
With the heliotrope or the mignonette?
With forget-me-not blue as the summer sky,
Looking up modestly with her gold eye?
Fair queen, I never can guess it I'm sure,
Unless 'tis the drooping lily pure.

QUEEN.

What is that flower that grows 'neath the hedges,
Or by the brooklet's bright green edges?
She is as blue as the ocean wild,
Modest, meek, tender, lovely and mild,
Beautiful flower! world-renowned,
With that and no other shall my brow be crowned.

[Title of a Book to be filled for Mama's Birthday.]

A FEW

𝕸𝖔𝖘𝖘𝖊𝖘 𝖆𝖓𝖉 𝕾𝖍𝖊𝖑𝖑𝖘

FROM

𝕷𝖎𝖑𝖞 𝕸𝖆𝖞'𝖘 𝕮𝖆𝖇𝖎𝖓𝖊𝖙,

Dedicated to

MY LOVING PARENTS,

Who kindly helped me to gather them together.

July 29, 1871.

INTRODUCTION

I WANDERED in the forest's cooling shade,
I sat beside the brooklet in the glade;
When, hearing some slight rustle, turned around
And saw a simple child upon the ground.
Pushed back were her curly golden ringlets,
And her eyes the hue of the violets.
She saw me not, but spoke this simple word,
Nor knew that any one had overheard.

CHILD.

Oh! prattling mountain brook that flowest calm
Bepast the meadow green or peaceful farm,
I'm sure thou hast some secret yet untold,
I prythee, brooklet, it to me unfold,
For thou dost chatter most mysteriously,
And whisper often to the old oak tree
And laugh, and spatter water over me.

BROOK.

I have a secret, truly hast thou said;
I have a secret, gentle little maid;
I have a secret I'd to none disclose
But to my innocent, my gentle rose.
Dost see the pebbles on my bosom there?
Dost see the mosses on the old oak tree?
Upon each stone a tale is written, rare,
And many a tale the moss will tell to thee;
For books in running brooks are, one has said,
And sermons in the pebbles smooth are laid.

CHILD.

I thank thee, brooklet, I'll come every day
And read the tales so carefully hid away.
And then she tripped off to her little farm,
Swinging her hat with bare, plump, snowy arm.
I took some stones, and moss from off the tree,
And many a tale the moss has told to me,
And many tales from off the stones I've read,
And for that day I always have been glad;
And so I wrote, for you to read, this book,
And ever will I praise the running brook.

The Child and the Brook.

(Dedicated to my friend, "Cousin Fanny.")

August, 1871.

CHILD.

BROOKLET, brooklet! where hast thou
    been?

BROOK.

I've been dancing in the woodland glen;
I rushed down the lofty mount so fleet;
I serenaded the forget-me-nots sweet;
I stopped at the foot of the hill to dally,
And kiss the lily of the valley.

CHILD.

Brooklet, brooklet! what heardest thou?

BROOK.

I heard the birds sing above on the bough,
I heard the sea murmur a lullaby;
To the silvery moon in the star-lit sky,
Heard a nightingale mourn her love-melody.

CHILD.

Brooklet, brooklet! what didst thou see?

BROOK.

I saw the violets nodding to me,
And a squirrel cracking nuts in a tree ;
I saw the fays dance on the mountain-tops,
I watered the golden butter-cups ;
I saw the fringèd gentian blue,
And new-born roses bathed in dew,
But the best that I've seen, little maiden, is you !

Our Johnnie.

August 30, 1871.

OH ! who loves not our Johnnie,
  Our baby, our little pet?
He is the greatest treasure,
  That ever we've had yet.

He came to us when the roses
  Did twine the porch around,
When the robin sang his sweetest,
  And the cricket made cheerful sound.

But dearer to me than the roses,
  Than the robin full of joy,
Than the cricket that chirps so merrily,
  Is my own Johnnie baby-boy.

With his fair snow-white complexion,
  With his nut-brown hair and eyes,
With his innocent, hearty laughter,
  And his little mannikin size.

Oh, precious gem of childhood !
How little dost thou know
Of the anxious cares of a mother,
And of sorrow's dreaded flow.

Oh Lord ! preserve this our treasure,
And let him live to be grown,
Let him be our comfort and pleasure,
And let Thy will be his own.

An Evening Landscape; or My View.

September 5, 1871.

MY window looks out to the west
   Where stretches the mountain wide,
Beneath it the river blue,
   So pure and calm doth glide.

I sat alone by the window,
   And it was nigh to eve,
When I saw the prospect beautiful
   I scarce could my eyes believe.

The smiling sun was descending
   Behind the mountain old,
Sinking from clouds of crimson
   And leaving a train of gold.

It smiled on the peaceful river,
   It fringed the ripples with light,
And gently smiled on the dim-lit earth,
   And bade each thing good-night.

The river murmured softly,
　The cows for milking lowed,
While on the peaceful shadowy lake
　A new-made couple rowed.

There was many a little cottage,
　And farm-house with age brown,
There was many a little village,
　And the view of many a town.

The sun saw itself reflected
　In the waters of the lake,
At the sight it blushingly sank below,
　And its evening rest did take.

The cottager sate at supper,
　And from work trod the weary men,
And the birds' evening songs reëchoed
　From mountain unto glen.

Then night stole soft the horizon,
　And threw her mantle round,
And the daisy closed its golden eye,
　And there was not a sound.
　8*

Then the little stars peeped shyly
  Through night's robe, one by one,
And flashed their lamps athwart the sky
  To light the path of the moon.

Then suddenly o'er the star-lit sky
  There issued a brighter light,
And the silver-robed moon with watchful eye
  Smiled forth upon the night.

And then from the gates of heaven
  The guardian angel fled,
And stole to the little cottage,
  For the children had gone to bed.

Then she and the moon watched over
  The children all the night,
And from the angel's starry crown
  There issued the brightest light.

And the children now are sleeping
  'Neath their tender motherly care,
And they dream the sweetest of earthly dreams,
  And they sleep without a fear.

"Handsome Is that Handsome Does;" or The Three Flowers.

September 5, 1871.

IT was at night; I slept and dreamed a dream,
A fair white form stood by me, did it seem;
It beckoned, glided off, I followed it,
'Neath the night-mantled sky did we two flit;
And in the cypress and the orange grove,
And wood, and dewy meadow, did we rove.

I saw a gate; within, a garden was
In which bloomed many flowers beauteous;
And I did wonder when I saw more, plain
Bloom in the handsome flowers' stately train.
My guide then smiled, and plucked some flowers too,
One gay pink, one red, one plain purplish blue.

He smiled, and said to me, " now take thy choice ;"
I plucked the rose, the gay one beauteous,
When on a sudden it my hand did prick,
I threw it on the pathway very quick,
And said, " ungrateful is the handsome rose,
Alas ! how very vainly did I choose !"

I said, " I'll choose chrysanthemum red, then
For smooth and thornless is its simple stem ;"
I plucked it, smelt it, oh ! its nauseous smell,
I let it go, and to the ground it fell.
" Ungrateful are all flowers " I said, " to me?"
He smiled and said, " Do thou but wait and see."

" Then I must take this plain blue violet,"
I sadly said, " though it cannot be sweet."
I took it, smelt of it, oh ! sweet it smelt !
I joyfully did place it in my belt.
And said, oh, why did I this one refuse ?
Oh, why did I those handsome vain ones choose ?"

" A thousand, thousand times, within my eyes,
This modest, gentle flower beautifies
Itself, and seems to me more beauteous !"
He smiled and said, " 'Tis handsome, handsome does ;
Know thou my name is meek humility,
This humble flower an emblem is of me."

Then I awoke, and found I'd dreamed at night,
And so for you my dream in rhyme did write,
Hoping you'd learn a lesson possibly,
Not to love things that handsome are to see,
For as you older grow you soon will learn
That outward handsome things do often turn ;
Humility is really beauteous,
As you will find, " 'tis handsome, handsome does."

The Evening Scene.

October 11, 1871.

THE weary traveler paused at mountain-top,
And for a moment rested on his staff;
But oh! how dear that scene was to his eyes!
Far in the west in splendor set the sun,
While the pale moon, impatient for her turn
To shine above, on throne in watchful light,
Hovered about, peeping betwixt wee clouds.
In the dim distance lay his native town.
He seemed to see the little cottage neat;
He seemed to see inside the flickering fire,
While round it gathered a home-circle true—
Brothers and sisters, buxom, loving, sweet;
He seemed to hear the knitting needles' click,
Tremblingly plied by the industrious hand
Of his dear mother, old and silver-haired,
While in most trembling accents read his sire
The evening paper to his listening wife.
He seemed to hear the crowing of the babe.

Not all however in that circle were.
One slept beneath the willow by the brook,
Another had a circle of her own,
And Jamie on the battle-field did sleep.
Down in the valley gleamed the river blue,
Dotted with many a white-winged ship,
While here and there a little light shone dim
Through the thick veil of many tow'ring trees.
Just then the moon, impatient, had her wish,
And the sweet sun in brilliant wonders set.
Then night stole forth and rolled the curtain down,
And from his eyes was shut the lovely scene.

Linda and the Brook.

(Dedicated to my dear Father on his Birthday.)

October 12, 1871.

WHERE Linda sat beneath the trees,
  Where sighed the sweet-voiced mournful breeze,
A sweet voice on the silence broke,
And thus to gentle Linda spoke:
  " Fair maiden, come away with me
And I will carry thee under the sea;
Show thee the huge sea-castles old,
Where on his throne sits the sea-king bold.
I will comb thy hair with a comb of pearl—
Come with me beautiful, beautiful girl!
I'll curl around me thy beautiful locks,
As at midnight sit we on the rocks;
When come forth the graceful syrens and sing,
And form in the sea a graceful ring,
And dance and sing a sweet, sweet lay,
While 'twixt the rocks the mermaids play;
And from under her shining golden crown
Wondering the vesper-star looks down.

I will kiss thee, and kiss thee, and kiss thee oft,
While we list to the song of the syrens soft.
Fair gentle maiden come with me—
Why, gentle Linda, dost thou flee?
    Come with me, come with me,
    Under the sea!"

For days the brooklet called in vain,
For days he called her again and again,
Till he won the heart of Linda fair,
And under the sea he carried her.
And he kissed her, and kissed her, and to death he
    kissed her,
And sadly he wept, and sadly missed her,
And 'tis said at twelve, some time of the year,
That fishermen him calling her can hear.

To my Mother on her Birthday.

A MERRY, happy birthday
  I wish you, mother dear,
The day of your birth has come again,
  Bringing wealth and mirth and cheer.

Another year has left its print
  Upon the scroll of time;
It is stealing away your youth, mother,
  It is stealing away your prime.

But it cannot steal away your love,
  It cannot fathom your heart,
With the choice rich treasures you've laid up there
  You will never, never part.

May God spare you many a happy year
  For me upon this earth,
To cheer our little household,
  To brighten our little hearth.

May many rich golden pleasures
  For you be now in store,
I wish you a merry birthday,
  And I wish you many more.

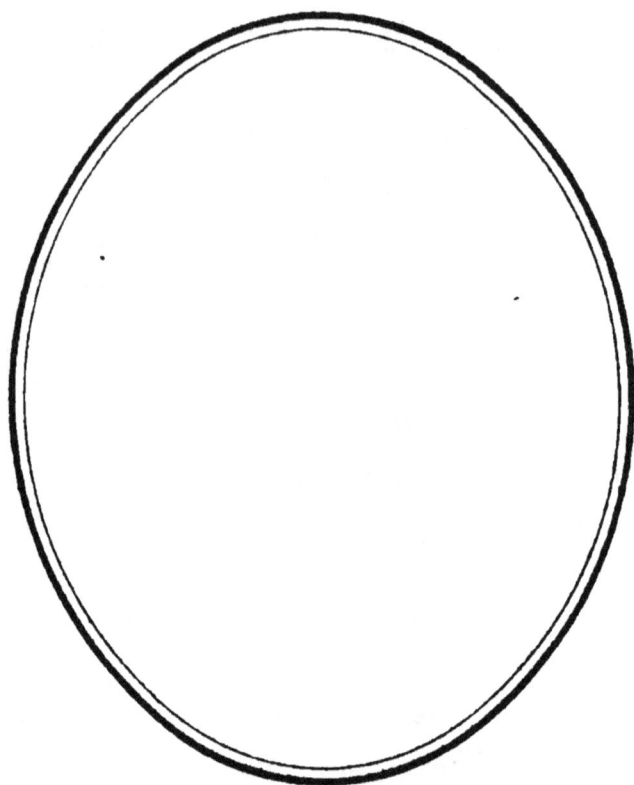

Hanna; or the Lovely Picture.

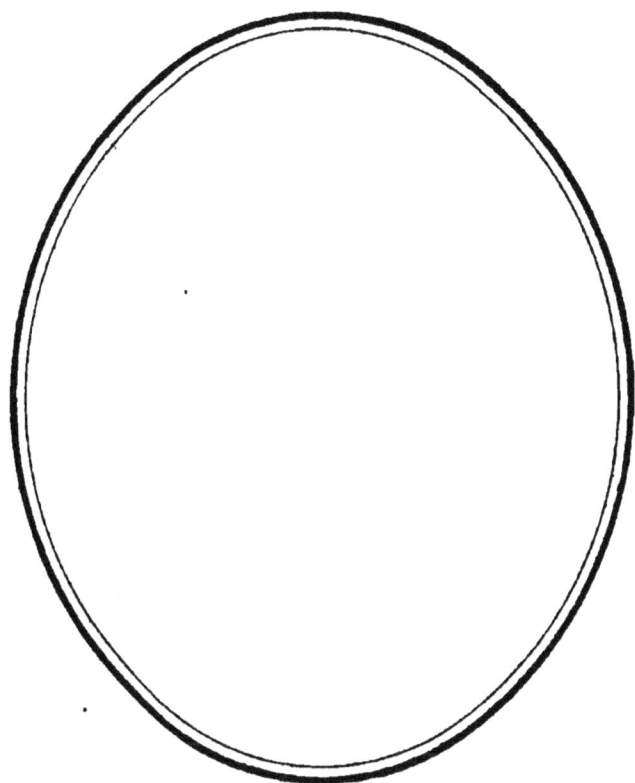

Yanna; or the Lovely Picture.

(Begun April 15 ; finished June 3, 1871.)

I.

INTRODUCTION.

SWEET Yanna! gentle maiden of the wild,
Blushing as rose, and beautiful as night,
With long black hair and dreamy azure eyes ;
Where'er thou stepped'st didst thou shed forth light !
She was the daughter of a king, his pride, his hope ;
She was his blossom, gem, heart, antelope.
She was as gay as red-breast robin was,
Her eyes did dazzle as the fire-fly glows.
9*

II.

THE CHANGE.

But days flew on, and gentle Yanna changed;
No longer sang she blithely as the thrush,
No longer skippêd on the grassy plain,
But spent her days alone, and thoughtful grew.
Now Ferdinand, her father, troubled was,
And sought to make her open forth her heart,
And tell him all that lay within its depths,
But 'twas in vain. She seemed to shun e'en him,
And sought her way to distant forest realms.

III.

THE PICTURE.

But youths and maidens, all who read will ask
What troubled her. 'Twas this—she pined for love!
The father troubled was, and every day
His wishes grew the more to know what 'twas.
But *what* she wanted scarcely did she know,

But that she wanted love's pure gentle flow.
Her father thought to turn her sadness off,
And cared for her with tender loving care.
One day, from town a little way, he took
Her to a show of pictures.   For he said,
" 'Twill please her.   I do long for the sweet ring
Of her gay laughter, and her merry smile."
One picture moved her strangely,   It was " Love,"
A youth and maiden 'neath the orange grove ;
Her long black ringlets sweeping to the ground,
He clasping her, she clasping him—and oh ! his eyes,
So brown ! so lustrous ! oh, so fondly did they shine !
Gazing at her ; and Cupid soared on high,
Chuckling and laughing, with his tiny bow
Grasped tight within his chubby elfin hands !
The tears rolled quickly down fair Yanna's cheek,
Her father was afeared and troubled sore ;
But as they wended on their way he saw
She was relieved, although he knew not how

IV.

THE WISH.

And then her father said, " I'll grant thy wish
If thou once more wilt merry, happy be."
Then Yanna thought, and said, " father, I will
If thou wilt grant the picture that we saw."
" What picture ?" quoth he, " Innocence or Joy ?"
" No, father! ' Love,' dost not remember that ?"
" Love ! by my faith," he said, " is nought but that
In this wide world to please a maid so fair
As Yanna! gentle, meek as violet ?"
" That, and no other wish I," Yanna said.
The father troubled looked.   " There is," quoth he,
" Plenty of gold, gay dresses, jewelry
No end.   One half my kingdom I'll grant thee."
The maiden hesitated not.   " I want
Not these," quoth she.   " That picture, that alone.
Send out thy courtiers o'er the world to find
That picture.   Never merry will I be
Till I see it.   Then will I be as blithe,
Merry, and gay as robin in the tree."

" But," said her father, " how'll we find it ? where ?"

" Give all thy money, if for me dost care."

" Then," said he, " I do consent, sweet maid,

For thy sake and for mine."

V.

THE DEPARTURE.

Then Ferdinand called all his courtiers round,

And said, " now each go mount your milk-white steeds,

And speed you to the master of the show

And buy of him the picture called ' Love.' "

Then all among themselves were much amazed,

And said, " He to fair Italy has gone."

" Then if it needs be to the end of earth !

Go, then, and not return till ye have it.

Here, take this money," counting thousands twelve.

" At your bidding," said they, and retired.

VI.

THE VOICE.

A twelve-month passed, a twelve-month came, and still
No trace of them was known, and Yanna fair
Used oft to sit and weep beside the rill.
One day sitting upon the violets rare,
Weeping and thinking that they'd ne'er return,
She heard a voice, and sweet and low it said—
" Why does this maiden weep among the fern,
Upon this flowery, grassy, shady bed ?"
" Who art thou ?" Yanna cried, " that speakest so ?"
The voice so low replied : " Thou must not know,
But I will be thy guide
If thou wilt promise me to strict obey."
" I will," sweet Yanna faint did say.
Then said the voice, "go and be gay,
Poor Ferdinand go cheer ;
Thou know'st thou promised to obey,
So shed not one more tear."
So Yanna rose and to the castle went,
The rest of that day merrily was spent,

And when at even did she go abed,
" I ne'er felt better for long time," she said.

VII.

THE RETURN.

One day when Ferdinand and Yanna, now
No longer sad, but gay as bird on bough,
Were straying in the forest, field and dale,
While blue birds' songs did float upon the gale ;
The little brook that gurgled at their feet
Did sing such harmonies that were as sweet
As blackbirds singing after summer rain,
Pouring and swelling their sweet songs in every vein,
When, suddenly, a trumpet loud did sound,
A cry sprang up, " The picture fair *is found*?"
Then Yanna, heeding not her father, sprang as fleet,
And sped away, as quickly moved her feet
As the graceful antelope, when in the chase
Moves 'long so fleetly and with so much grace.
" Give it to me," she cried, as up she came.

" 'Tis heavy for you," quoth a page, " good dame."

" Heavy for me !" she cried, "the thing that I

Oft used to weep for, oft for used to sigh—

Here ! do as I command you, instantly !"

She clasped the lovely picture to her breast,

And let no creature touch it even, lest

It should be stolen by some evil one,

And ran as fleet as if shot by a gun

Into the forest, and within its realm.

When out of sight, paused for a rest

Down on the mossy heath, beneath an elm

That stretched its roots as if to chair its guest.

VIII.

THE DREAM.

And Yanna, thinking she would rest awhile,

Soon in sweet slumber gently did beguile,

And dreamed of what before she dreamed ne'er ;

It was so soothing, wild, romantic, fair.

She dreamt she was in terror of an asp,

Just ready to give up in one last gasp,
When through the forest burst a noble youth,
(On his fair face shone beauty, love and truth,)
And killed it with one thrust of his sharp sword.
He turned to her, and took her on right straight
Unto her welcome, open castle gate.
Then Yanna woke, the lovely dream did end,
And quickly on her pleasant way did wend,
For the bright sun was bidding all good night,
With one last look of rosy lustrous light.

IX.

THE HIDING PLACE.

When evening shades were gath'ring fast,
Sweet Yanna reached a spot at last
    Where thickly grew
    The violet blue,
Whose perfume on the wind was cast.
'Twas an open spot in the dense wildwood,
And there as 'twere a temple stood.
    Inside of it
    A score could sit.
10

It looked as if 'twas made to brood
And shelter those that lost their way
In April showers or storms of May.
  It looked, though small,
  Welcome to all
Who tired were, or went astray.
To Yanna, welcome 'twas indeed—
'Twas near a mile that she had flee'd.
  Tired she was
  A long way 'twas,
The maiden sorely rest did need.
Still with the picture at her breast,
A minute more she paused for rest
  Upon the floor.
  The open door
Full welcome seemed to give its guest.—
But finally uprose again
With blood revived in every vein,
  Cheeks once more red,
  Away she sped,
Nor glance at beauty round did deign,
For she had seen it all before;
But opened quick a secret door,

Which showed a room with purple hung—
It seemed some ancient room of yore.
She pushed the heavy curtains back;
    An empty case
    Draped round with lace,
Hung up where beauty did not lack.
The lovely picture she put in
Away from misery and sin,
    From dirt and vice—
    She kissed it thrice,
There love and virtue reigned akin.
Then quick the curtains back she drew,
For night came on, and dark it grew,
    And sped away
    Quick's she could gae;
For though the path the maiden knew,
She knew the king would troubled be
If not his daughter did he see
Before night's shades hung o'er the lea.
But strange the pathway seemed to grow,
And quicker did the maiden go,—
But hark! what is't that hisseth so?
And nearer now the branches crash,

A snake from 'mid the wood did flash,
Using its tail for sort of lash,
'Bout two feet round and ten feet long,
Ponderous was it, big and strong,
The maid was 'fraid 'twould do her wrong.

X.

THE DREAM REALIZED.

The snake when it did Yanna see,
Gave forth remonstrances of glee,
And lashed with tail its scaly side.
The maiden fair was terrified,
And frightened was and much dismayed.
When suddenly a thought arose,
She raised her eyes to heaven and prayed;
And when her trembling prayer did close
She heard a noise in the deep glade,
And there a noble youth did stand
In uniform, with sword in hand,
And 'neath him on a flowery bed

The furious snake lay stretched out dead.
The tears rolled down fair Yanna's cheek,
For thankfulness she could not speak ;
So full her heart with joy did swell
That swooning, to the ground she fell,
And never knew a thing until
The morning sun shone on the rill ;
And when the morning star did peep
Then did she wake as if from sleep.
She found herself upon her own white cot,
Though how she got there ever she knew not.
Neither was she alone, for near did stand
A page, ready to wait at hand.
She was about to rise from her white bed
When the page stopped her, " Thou art sick !" he said.
" Sick !" most indignantly did she cry,
" Who ever felt more well and blithe than I ?
But take this robe—how came it soiled so ?
Last night it was as white as fallen snow !"
" Dost not remember ?" cried the page, " last night
When thou with that fine picture took'st thy flight?
And how we found thee in the wood in swoon,
Close where the brooklet flowed with gurgling tune,
    10*

Where violets did make the ground so blue
That grasses and their leaves were very few,
There, where the robin sang his merry lay,
The dwelling-place of happy flow'ring May,
Who skips light-footed through the wood and field,
Who makes the innocents their blossoms yield,
Who breaks the chains of ice that bind the brook,
Who makes the violets spring in every nook.
Beside thee lay a snake, dead, with sides gored,
And o'er thee bent a youth with bow and sword.
We brought thee, swooning, pale, to thy home here,
And I have watched all night thy bedside near."
" And what did you with him? now tell me, lad "—
" Thy father," said the page, " was very mad,
And swore that if he did not leave the place
He'd meet him in a trial, face to face."
The maiden spake not.   Tears rolled down her cheek,
And when the page asked why, she could not speak.
" But hence, ye idle tears !" at length she cried,
And forthwith her sad trembling eyes she dried,
And skipped so gaily Ferdinand to meet,
With smile upon her face so blithe and sweet—

So fresh and merry did her laughter ring,
As if base sadness was an unknown thing.

XI.

THE DESPONDENCY.

But changes came; and now once more
A look of sadness Yanna wore;
She thought of the strong, noble youth,
And pined for him, to say the truth.
Her picture comfort was alone,
One day beside it she did moan,
She heard the *voice*, and sweet, sweet tone
Say, " why dost weep so sad and lone?
Did I not tell thee to obey?
Go, then, and cheer thy father's way;
Go, do it merrily with glee,
And always blithe and happy be."
The maid unwillingly arose,
Much she preferred to weep and drowse,
But still the voice did seem to say,
" Go thou, and cheer thy father's way."

XII.

THE MEETING AND THE SEPARATION.

One day while Yanna sat beneath the trees,
While flowers sweet did scent the passing breeze,
And Yanna sang so blithe and gay and sweet,
She paused on sudden, and her song did cease,
For hark! she hears the tramp of horse's feet,
Clattering, coming nearer, near.
Crackling branches she doth hear;
—Near her a branch cracked and out there came
The lad, the youth, the very same
That helped the lone and wandering maid,
Who, were it not for him, were dead.
With cry of joy then Yanna fair upsprang
And gazed at him.   He seemed the likeness of
The cherished picture Yanna had, called " Love ;"
When near did sound a horse's tramp,
A voice cried out, " Hi! you young scamp !" .
And quickly through the forest rode
King Ferdinand, with wrathful face,
And cried, as he his gun did load,

"Did I not tell thee—leave the place?
Then go, thou rogue; and if thou dost not leave
Before set in the shades of mourning eve,
I trow thou'lt sorry be for it, bold lad,
And I for it will make thee very sad;
Go! mount thy coal-black steed," he cried—
"I'll see to this," the youth replied;
But straightway on his saddle sate,
And quickened up his horse's gait,
And waving back his shining spear,
And wiping off a would-be tear,
He quickly in the forest sped,
For in the west the sun shone red.

XIII.

THE SERENADE.

'Tis midnight! all have gone to rest,
All, all in sweetest slumbers blest
Except one person, all do sleep.
'Tis Yanna! who alone doth weep,
Tossing so restless in her cot;

And she the only one is not,
For there a youth on coal-black steed
Doth toward the palace quickly speed,
And ties his noble charger tight—
That steed had witnessed many a fight,
And often quick had borne his charge
Through the dense forest at a large,
And often in a fight or fray
Had borne his master many a day,
By field and valley, dale or wood,
Scarce with a taste of any food.
'Twas a noble, prancing, coal-black steed
Which outdid every horse in speed ;
He but his master would obey,
Useful was he in fight or fray.
And then the youth with sweet guitar,
Beneath fair Yanna's window knelt,
Called forth such strains as now are rare,
To show the love he for her felt—
I'll tell the notes as they were told to me
By a daisy blooming near by on that lea.

The Serenade.

Gem of my bosom,
　　Fount of my heart,
Pearl of the ocean,
　　Why should we part?
Wanderers we are on this lone wide earth,
Thinking and hoping for future mirth.

Chorus.

O, come with me where the western wind's blowing,
Where the brooklet calm and cool is flowing,
Where primroses and violets bloom in the wood,
To render the honey-bee luscious food.

Thy eyes are of azure,
　　Thy hair Spaniard's dark,
And thy voice is as sweet
　　As the song of the lark.
O, come to me, dearest, together we'll roam,
O say, gentle Yanna, wilt be my own?

Chorus.

O come with me where the western wind's blowing,
Where the brooklet calm and cool is flowing,
Where primroses and violets bloom in the wood,
To render the honey-bee luscious food.

Thy breath is as sweet as the rose newly born,
Thy footstep as light as the graceful shy fawn,
Thy fair brow with roses is all intertwined,
While their scent floats afar on the whispering wind.
Fair fountain, gem, antelope, pearl, rose, my dove!
O come with me darling, my own true love,
Where the nightingale sings a serenade
To the violet in the wild green glade,
Where the butterfly floats on the dancing wing,
Where the oak trees gaunt shadows on the green moss fling;
There heavy laden are the green trees with fruit,
There will I play to thee on the flute.
Then haste to me darling, make no stay,
For over the skies hangs morn's dusky gray!

The maiden sprang from her window low,
And he caught her in his arms below,

And he mounted her on his prancing steed
And they were about from the castle to speed,
When they heard a rustle and looking around,
They saw standing ghost-like upon the gronnd,
With enraged face, king Ferdinand
With his faithful page, and his sword in hand.
" What, thou again !" he said, " thou hindering youth,
I'm tired of thee, to say the truth.
Now look ye here, if 'fore the clock strikes nine
Thou be not 'cross the waters of the Rhine,
I'll send my warriors after thee so bold,
And for a year in prison thee I'll hold,—
Come maiden, come with me."

XIV.

THE CAPTURE.

Although the youth's horse gallopped quick,
Although he spared not spur and whip,
School bells did chime,
The clock struck nine
Before he'd cleared the woodland strip.

11

The warriors on their saddles sate,
And gallopped with a quickened gait,
  Though the youth too
  Nigh almost flew,
And gallopped quick, but 'twas too late.
They bore him to the jail near by,
There for a twelve month did he lie.
  Alone in jail,
  He did bewail
For a long year, till him they'd try.

 * * * * * *

XV.

THE BANQUET AND TOURNAMENT.

And now the father looked at Yanna fair,
And said, " She needs a gallant, valiant youth
Who will protect her in life's dreary way,
Who'll make her bright and blithe, and cheer her up."
And so he made a banquet in the hall,
And all the gallant youths did thereto call,
And all the knights, princes, and warriors brave,

Did gather round the board most merrily.
After the feast, king Ferdinand arose
And said, " Now come forth knights and warriors brave ;
Now who shall conquer all the others most
Shall win the lily of fair Germany.
Then forth came prancing on a milk-white steed
A gallant warrior, robed in dazzling white,
And said, " There ne'er was braver, bolder squire
Than Robert William, of fair Germany."
Then forth there came upon a coal-black steed,
(That seemed to outdo every horse in speed,)
A youth who though in suit of mail was clad,
Still Yanna thought she knew those features bold—
Although she was not sure, and trembled much.
They drew their coursers up within the ring,
Then, bowing low, the action did begin.
Long, long they fought, the milk-white and the black,
Neither did boldness, strength, nor courage lack.
But see ! the milk-white steed is overthrown,
The coal-black has the first one bravely won.
And one by one the knights so bravely fought,
And one by one unto the ground were brought.
And then the last, a dappled monster, came,

Throughout all Germany was spread his fame,

And none were known more brave and strong than he,

His bold, brave face, e'en men shuddered to see.

For full an hour did the duel last.

And then upon the ground with face aghast

Lay the gray steed—and fainting and so white,

Stretched at full length the conquered knight.

Then did the heavens re-echo joyful shouts,

Roses were scattered in the victor's route,

And the victorious wreath his fair hair graced,

By Yanna's snowy hand was it there placed.

Then Yanna said, " Father, I do request

That we be married in the wood, within

The little temple in the flowery glen."

" But why," he said, " should you be married there ?

Than there, I'd have you married anywhere !"

But as he loved the maid exceedingly

He did consent at last, to their great glee.

XVI.

THE MARRIAGE.

Then did the bridal train proceed

With Yanna on a milk-white steed ;

Beside her on coal-black did speed
The youth with waving emerald plumes ;
Behind them rode bridesmaids and grooms.
The heavy curtains back were drawn,
Upon the secret nails were hung,
And the fair picture callèd " Love,"
Did hang the bridal pair above.
The maiden gazed at the picture fair,
To see if she could get knowledge there
As to whether the youth was her own true knight ;
Cupid seemed to nod as if she were right.
Then tremblingly she took his hand,
She scarcely knew where she did stand.
Then they lifted the warrior's armor off,
The maiden looked—'twas her own true love.

XVII.

THE RECOGNITION.

Then Ferdinand saw it was Edward Lisle,
The fairest earl there was in Germany.
They once had known each other in their youth.
   11*

Then down upon his knees fell Ferdinand
And begged the pardon of the gracious earl,
Who did it graciously I you assure.

XVIII.

THE DEPARTURE.

" And now we must away," at length said he—
' But where is Yanna?   I do not her see !"
They looked, but could not see where she had gone,
Till they bethought she to the wood had flown ;
And sure enough, they met her in the wood,
Running beside the brooklet's babbling flood,
With something clasped tightly to her heart
As if she did not mean with it to part.
Then they on white and coal-black steeds,
Did trample through the whispering reeds
That rustle, quiver round the river Rhine,
Oft mingled with the bluebird's sphery chime.
'Twas midnight when they reached those waters clear.
A sight that e'en to lab'ring men is dear.
No ripple stirred those placid waters blue,

In Germany e'en such scenes are very few.
The weeping willow clasped those waters calm,
And sweetly scented was the air with balm ;
From out her window looked the moon on high,
And gazed on them with pensive, smiling eye.
Then they dismounted from their coursers bold,
(The sight has splendor more than halls of gold.)
He led her to those waters clear and fair,
She looked, and saw herself reflected there—
The blushing cheeks, those eyes of azure blue,
Such maidens in the world are very few.
She blushed, and hid her face upon his breast,
Alone together did the couple rest,
Alone, sweet word, may it be blest.

XIX.

THE CASTLE.

The dusky gray of dawn was spreading fast,
When, tired, they reached the welcome spot at last,
And to the maiden's great delight it stood
Within a little, shady, flowering wood,

Quite o'ergrown with the rose and eglantine,
Close by the waters of the placid Rhine.
And there alone with him she did abide,
Constant companions, he her love and guide.
Sir Edward was a painter, you must know,
He tried to teach sweet Yanna so to do.

XX.

THE PICTURE.

One day as they were roaming in the vale,
While flowers sweet did scent the passing gale,
While his fair brow with roses sweet was graced,
A wreath that Yanna wove, and had there placed,
He said to her, " Thou never to me told,
The thing thou keepest sacred more than gold,
The thing thou keepest locked up in thy breast,
Tell me! until I know I will not rest."
" Yes," said the maiden fair, " and so I will,
But keep it secret, and to no one tell.
It is a picture fair, and as you said,
I prize it more than gold or rubies red,

And here it is!"   She plucked it from her breast.
He gazed upon the picture so cherished—
" What, then!" he cried, " is it the very same
That I myself did paint?   What! that again?
Yes! 'tis the same! the very same!
Yes! 'tis the same! there is the blotted line!
When this I painted, I for love did pine."
And still the youth and maid lived happily,
And if more of them ever do I see
I'll tell it all to thee.

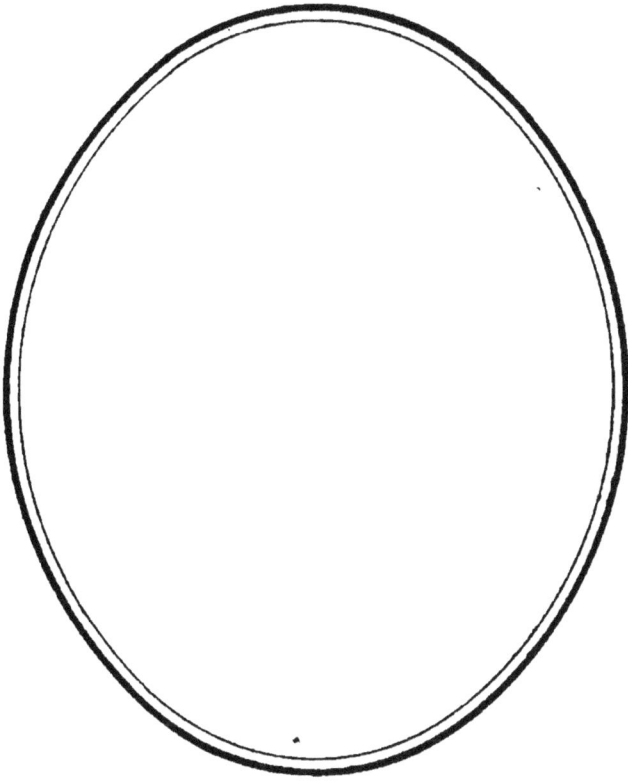

Dramas.

A Rolling Stone Gathers no Moss.

A TRAGEDY.

February 21, 1871.

Dramatis Personæ.

SIRIUS, Duke of Naples, enemy to Herold.

ATLANTA, Daughter of Sirius.

HEROLD, Lover of Atlanta.

EGLANTINE, Queen of Fairies.

> BALSAM,
> IVY,
> SNOWBLOSSOM,
> ROSEBUD,
> } Fairies attending on Queen.

ORANUS, An evil spirit.

DARING, His servant.

> SCENE, *Naples, a wood near by.*

12

ACT I.

SCENE 1.—*A room in* SIRIUS' *palace.* ATLANTA *and* HEROLD *together.*

Atlanta. Hearken! Hither comes my father!

(*Enter* SIRIUS. *Exeunt* HEROLD *and* ATLANTA, *running.*)

Sirius. The brute! the beast! I'll have him yet. (*Sits down.*) Ha! Ha! Ha! The brute! (*falls asleep, muttering,*)—You young hound! you hound, you!

(*Curtain falls.*)

ACT II.

SCENE 1.—*The Wood.*

Enter SIRIUS *and attendants.*)

Sirius. Come, go away, and leave me to my solitude.

(*Exeunt attendants.*)

(SIRIUS *lies down on moss—sleeps. Enter* EGLANTINE *and train.*)

Eglantine. Ha! a mortal on our private dancing ring! Make yourselves invisible!

(*Fairies draw spider-web cloaks about them.*)

Sirius (*in his sleep.*) The brute! the brute! Away with him!

Eglantine.   Ha! ha! ha! here is work for us!

(*Enter* ORANUS *with* DARING.   *Sweet music is heard.*)

Eglantine.   Hark! I hear the bridal bells of the lily of
the valley.   (*Exeunt* EGLANTINE *and train, singing.*)

> Far o'er the blue mountain,
> Beside the clear fountain,
> 'Neath the violets sweet
> Speed our queer elfin feet.

Oranus.   Ha! ha! ha!

SCENE 2.—*The same.*

Enter EGLANTINE *and train.*

Eglantine.   (*to Ivy, singing.*)
> O'er the meadow grasses sweet,
> Quickly speed your elfin feet,
> Sprinkle this in Sirius' eyes
> When upon his couch he lies.

(*Gives a bottle.   Exit* IVY, *singing.*)

Ivy.   Who can quicker run than I?
> With pretty golden wings I fly;
> My eyes are sharp and gray and keen,
> Among the forest trees I'm seen.

ACT III.

SCENE 1.—*A room in* SIRIUS' *castle—Evening—*SIRIUS *sleeping on couch.*

Enter IVY, *sprinkles from bottle in* SIRIUS' *eyes. Exit singing.*

Ivy.—Henceforth, now, he will adore him,
Choose him from all men before him.

SCENE 2.—*A room in* SIRIUS' *castle—*ATLANTA *and* HEROLD—SIRIUS *having been changed in the night.*

Sirius. Yes, I give my free consent. Take her and be happy!

(*Exeunt* HEROLD *and* ATLANTA, *rejoicing.* SIRIUS *lies down, falls asleep, says,*)

Sirius. Fair Herold! take her, good man! be happy!

(*Enter* DARING *with bottle, sprinkles something in* SIRIUS' *eyes. Exit.*)

SCENE 3.—*A Church.* ATLANTA *and* HEROLD *being married.*

Enter SIRIUS, *having been changed again by the evil spirit —Rushes forth, drags out* ATLANTA, *shouting—A general uproar.* (*Curtain falls.*)

ACT IV.

SCENE 1.—*A court of justice—Judge, officers, etc.*—SIRIUS *sitting with judge. Enter attendants bringing* HEROLD.

Sirius (severely.) What meantest thou, when thou tookest Atlanta?

Herold. My lord, I had your free consent.

Sirius. The witch! the vile wretch! (*To attendants,*) take him away, and keep him close! (*Exeunt.*)

ACT V.

SCENE 1.—*A prison—*HEROLD *discovered chained, sitting disconsolately.*

Herold. Oh, my Atlanta, see me! see me!

(*A song is heard. Enter* ROSEBUD *with key, delivers it to* HEROLD, *singing.*)

Rosebud. Fear not Herold, young and brave,
Take this key and you 'twill save.

(*Exit* ROSEBUD. HEROLD *unlocks door and is free.*)
12*

SCENE 2.—*The wood.*

Enter SIRIUS *and* HEROLD *at opposite doors.*

Sirius—(*proudly.*)   Fight me if you dare !   A stronger
man than I is not in Naples !

(*They fight.* HEROLD *stabs* SIRIUS, *who falls. Exit*
HEROLD. *Enter* EGLANTINE *and train. They bear*
SIRIUS *away, singing.*)

> Here is the once proud Sirius,
>> Who toward his mournful end
> Was very near delirious,
>> And haunted by a fiend.

ACT VI.

SCENE 1.—*A church*—ATLANTA *and* HEROLD *being*
married.

Enter EGLANTINE *and train, singing,*

You'll prosper and have splendid health,
With riches, beauty, friends and wealth.

(*Curtain falls*

No Use Crying for Spilled Milk.

A TRAGEDY.

April, 1871.

———

Dramatis Personæ.

HESPERUS, Prince of Liberia; lover of Camilla.

HERCULES, His brother, lover of Camilla.

CAMILLA, Countess of Venice, love to Hercules.

SICKLES, Servant of Hesperus.

STILLWATERS, A Clown.

CUPID, A Fairy Sprite.

    Station Master, Conductor, Passengers in cars.

    Town Boys.

    A dog belonging to Station Master.

SCENE, *Sometimes in Venice, sometimes in Liberia.*

ACT I.

SCENE 1.—*A wood near Venice.* CAMILLA *lying on the moss beside a brook.*

Camilla. Fain would I drown myself beneath thy flood,
Fain fill thy waters all with fallen tears.
Enter HESPERUS.

Hesperus. Why greet'st thou, fair Camilla? why beside
This brooklet's cool and babbling, rippling flow,
Answer me, dearest, what doth trouble thee?

Camilla. 'Tis nought but folly, do not ask me, pray.

Hesperus. Ah! but I shall before I go away.
Enter SICKLES.

Sickles. I'm bid to hail you to dinner.　　(*Exeunt.*)

SCENE 2.—*A room in Camilla's palace.* CAMILLA *and* HESPERUS *together.*

Hesperus. Why doubting, dearest? come to me, oh do!
From every hurtful thing I'll shelter you.

Camilla—(*rising.*)　Propose, oh do not! for my heart is
sore!
Oh haughty Hesp'rus do not to me more!
　　　　　　　　　　(*Exit.*)

Hesperus—(*pacing the floor.*)   Sad fate for me!
  Pale sorrow stares me in the face
  With ghostly looks and countenance so base.
                    (*Curtain falls.*)

SCENE 3.—*A wood near Venice.* CAMILLA *lying on the
                    moss. Enter* CUPID.

Cupid.   I dance upon the brooklet's foam,
          Among the tree-tops do I roam,
          Upon the rushing wind I ride,
          In sweet primroses do I hide.
          Flowers spring up where'er I go,
          I wing the forest to and fro,
          I court the gentle nymphs at eves,
          For me the moss a carpet weaves.
          Who is a happier fay than I,
          So gay, so nimble, and so shy?
                    (*Discovers* CAMILLA.)
          Who be this that lieth here,
          On her cheek a fallen tear?
      Ah, it is Camilla!   I am invisible.
      (*Draws a cloak of butterfly wings about him.*)

Camilla—(*to herself.*)   Propose, oh do not! for my heart
    is sore !

    Oh haughty Hesp'rus, do not to me more.

Cupid.   Ha! ha! ha! I will fix her.

            (*Dances around* CAMILLA, *singing,*

    Now in sleep, Camilla fair,

    Close thine eyelids white and rare,

    Dream of love, and not of care.

    Hesp'rus shall win thee to his heart,

    For I will fire the lover's dart !

(CAMILLA *sleeps*—CUPID *fires dart—Exit* CUPID—*Enter*

    HESPERUS—*In a few minutes* CAMILLA *awakes.*)

Camilla.   Where am I? and who art thou ?

    Or is it but a swaying bough ?

Hesperus.   Dost know me not, my pride, my love ?

    Oh list to me, my cooing dove !

Camilla.   What thou ? and what dost here alone ?

Hesperus.   The same question I myself am inclined to ask.

Camilla.   I was but roaming 'neath the forest trees,

    And listening to the humming of the bees ;

    I laid me down upon this soft green moss

    Where I could watch the brooklet's silvery source,

    And here I slumbered, and dreamt such a dream

That never have I had, it now doth seem ;
I should have slumbered longer 'neath this oak,
But you came, so from dreamland I awoke.
Hesperus.   Come, dear, and with me now forever roam,
And I will take thee to Liberia home.
Camilla.   I do consent; I give you this ring; keep it,
and remember me.

ACT II.

Scene 1.—*Liberia.*

(*A depot, cars just stopping, passengers get out, among them* Camilla *and* Hesperus. Hesperus *drops ring. Exeunt cars, passengers, station master, etc.; dog stays behind—Enter* Town Boys, *laughing, shouting, and kicking each other—Dog digs in hole—barks.*)

1st *Boy.*   Here Carlo ! Carlo ! Carlo !
2d *Boy.*   A rat, perhaps.
3d *Boy.*   I'll go and see.
(*Peeps into hole—calls to others—holding up gold ring, shouts,*

A ring ! a gold ring !

1st Boy. A likely story.

2d Boy. Let us go and see!

(*Runs up to* 3D BOY, *shouts, the others follow—they quarrel over the ring. Enter* SICKLES.)

Sickles. What meaneth this?

Boys. A ring! a ring!

Sickles. Give it me. (*They give ring.*)

That be my master's, and no other.

Boys (*all together.*) Give it me!

Sickles. I will not.

(*Exit* SICKLES, *pursued by* BOYS.)

ACT III.

SCENE 1.—*Liberia, a room in* HESPERUS' *palace.* HESPERUS *on a Couch.*

Hesperus. Now come to me, thou ring of gold,

My charge I'll keep, my charge I'll hold.

What ho! not here! what fate!

What meaneth it? Has it disappeared? (*Rings.*)

Enter STILLWATERS.

Hesperus. Hast seen a ring?

Stillwaters. A ring? Of course, who has not?

Hesperus (*impatiently.*) I mean a ring dropped on the ground.

Stillwaters. Upon the ground? Certainly, at the circus.

Hesperus. There's none to be got from you!

Go find my trusty servant. (*Exit* STILLWATERS.)

Oh, cruel fate! oh, weeping I!
Oh, that to my love might I fly!
How can I tell her this sad news!
Oh, fate! sadly dost thou abuse!

Re-enter STILLWATERS.

Hast found him?

Stillwaters. He is nowhere to be seen.

Hesperus. Don't tell me that, thou rascal!

Till that ring be found. (*Exit* STILLWATERS.)

Enter CAMILLA.

Camilla. Dearest, how comest on?

(HESPERUS *shows hand.*)

What! didst not keep it! Then thou art not true to me. Oh Hesperus, when I first woke in that wood, I thought myself with one who loved me as his own soul.

(*Exeunt.*)

13

ACT IV.

SCENE 1.—*Liberia.   A room in the palace of* HERCULES.
HERCULES *alone.*

Hercules.   I'll taste not!   Oh, I'll drink not!
     Camilla, for love of thee;
   For e'er thy winning picture
     Haunteth so, still round me.
   I'll haste to my Camilla,
     Though winds may blow and howl,
   I'll win her to a full heart,
     The marriage bells shall toll.
                    (*Exit.   Curtain falls.*)

SCENE 2.—*Venice.   A room in* GAMILLA'S *palace.*
CAMILLA *alone.   Enter* HERCULES.

Hercules.   Oh Camilla! oh Camilla! if thou wouldst but
          come to me!
       Then Camilla! then my mistress! we parted shall
          never be!
Camilla.   Readily do I consent,
       Joyfully do I repent
          Of my former folly.

Oh that I had taken thee before,
None can ever love me more
    Than thou, Hercules!

Hercules. Then come with me.   (*Exeunt.*)

SCENE. 3.—*A church.* HESPERUS *and* CAMILLA
married.

ACT V.   .   ·

SCENE 1.—*Liberia. A room in* HESPERUS' *palace.*
HESPERUS *alone, weeping. Enter* SICKLES.

Sickles. The ring! the ring!

Hesperus. The ring! give it me!

Sickles. There is no hope. They are married!

Hesperus. Who?

Sickles. Camilla and Hercules.

Hesperus. Then is she lost to me? Then bring me
my sword.

  (*Sickles brings sword.* HESPERUS *stabs himself. Dies.*)
                   (*Curtain falls.*)

Victor, the King of Fairy-Land.

A Drama written for All-Hallow-e'en.

October, 1871.

Dramatis Personæ.

VICTOR, King of Fairy-Land.

NIGHTSHADE, an old Wizard, King of Gloom-Land.

GENU, King of Summer-Land.

JUNIOR, a Sylphid, bosom friend of Victor.

JEROLD, a Baron, father of Victor.

HYACINTH, a wealthy Count of Fairy-Land.

GAUNTLET, a Sylphid.

SLY, a Fairy Hunter, friend of Gauntlet.

BLANCHE, daughter of Count Hyacinth.

EVA, daughter of Victor.

A Congress, numerous Fairies, Sylphids, Soldiers, and Hunters.

SCENE, *Sometimes in Fairy-Land, sometimes in Summer-Land, sometimes in Gloom-Land, and sometimes in the air.*

ACT I.

SCENE 1.—*Fairy-Land. A wood. Curtain rises to a hunter's bugle.* KING VICTOR *and hunters. A song heard from without.*

Song.

Where the modest violet bloometh,
Where the zephyr she perfumeth,
Here I lie day after day,
Listing to the robin's lay.
Come quiet thought, fling care away,
Come sweet-voiced, laughing joy, so gay,
Come, come, come away,
And weave a gentle dream for me
While I slumber 'neath this tree.

Victor. Heard I the sweet-voiced robin's merry trill?
Heard I the gurgling of the mountain rill?
No such song issues from the robin's bill;
The rill's song never does my bosom fill
With such a strange, prophetic, sudden thrill,
Nor ever could, nor ever, ever will.
Hark! silence, hunters, list! I hear it still,
Stay there till I come back, which soon I will.

13*   (*Exit.*)

Scene 2.—*Curtain rises to soft music. Another part of the wood near by.* Blanche *asleep. Enter* Victor.

Victor.   What have we here? a sleeping angel fair?
  My kin do never have such silken hair.
  These thoughtful, meaning eyes are fairer far
  To have than my kinswomen ever dare.
  This truly is the sleeping beauty rare,
  But fairer, fairer than the prince found e'er.
  This form's too lovely for e'en fairy land.
  But o'er thee, vision sweet, too long I stand,
  Yet here's a violet for thy lily hand.
  Sweet melody, to you be well-a-day,
  'Tis dangerous, eaves-dropper, long to play.
                              (*Exit.*)

Blanche (*awakening.*)   What sprites have been here while
      I slumbered sweet?
  Hark! I do hear sounds of retreating feet!
  Who placèd in my hand this violet?
  Say, be it enemy, or be it friend?
  Be it a harmless fay, or evil fiend?
  I like not this.   It ne'er was so before,
  I am afeared, my heart is troubled sore.   (*Exit.*)

SCENE 3.—*Curtain rises to a hunter's bugle. The former part of the wood. Enter* KING VICTOR *and* HUNTERS, *among them* SLY.

King (*aside.*)   I will to see again that vision fair.
    (*aloud.*)   I'll soon come back, my hunters, stay you
        there.   (*Exit.*)
1*st Hunter.*   To me it seems the king doth favor hunting.
2*d Hunter.*   Aye; especially in this part of the wood.
Sly.   I would know what the good game be that our king
    delighteth in.
3*d Hunter.*   Which we have no part in.
Sly.   I've a mind to try my bow at that game.
Hunters.   Go.
Sly.   Aye, that I will.   (*Exit* SLY.)
1*st Hunter.*   He is the best to try that uncertain game, for
    sharper than his arrow is his eye, and soft and fleet
    his footstep as any lady fay.   (*Exeunt.*)

SCENE 4.—*The other part of the wood.   Curtain rises to
    soft music.   Enter* BLANCHE.

Blanche.   Now I'll lie as if in sweetest sleep,
    I'll close mine eyes in seeming slumbers deep,

But all the while a wakeful watch I'll keep.
To see if I the spirit can discover
    Who doth hover
    My bed over,
While I sleep amid the clover.

          (*Sings.*)

Where the bee so softly hummeth,
Where the little brooklet runneth,
I lie watching the sunbeam
In the brooklet's waters gleam ;
And I sleep in slumbers sweet,
While pleasant dreams my mind do greet.
              (*Seems to sleep.*)

      Enter VICTOR.

Victor.   Ah ! here's the tuneful robin in her nest,
    (*bending over her*)   Sweet songster, of all fays I love
    thee best.
Blanche.   Ha ! I have thee !
Victor.   What ho ! I thought thee asleep.
    Sweet songster of the wood, prithee, who art ?
Blanche.   I am the daughter of a Count,
    Hyacinth by name.   Dost recollect him ?

Victor.   I think I do.   He is a worthy fellow, if I rightly remember.

(*Enter* SLY *at a distance, concealed.*)

Blanche.   But say, who art thou that troublest my sleep?

Victor.   I would that voice were mine!

Blanche.   Tell me who art, thou bold, gay, gallant youth,
Or I'll bind thee with my strongest spell!

Victor.   Thy spells of no avail are.   I'm more strong
Than any at your command were wove.
Yet would I joy to be bound with a spell
Which was constructed from the sweet command
That issued from thy wind-like voice, fair lady.

Blanche.   Who art thou?   I am half afeared of thee!

Victor.   I am thy desparing, sighing lover sad.

Blanche.   Tell me who art, or I will flee from thee.

Victor.   Then I will out.   Thy king and lover I'm.

Blanche.   What didst thou say?   Thy name's not Victor, sure?

Victor.   Aye, that it is.   Come fairest, wilt be mine?

Blanche.   Oh, pardon! pardon! pardon! gracious king!

Victor.   Kneel not, but say, " Dearest, I will be thine."

Blanche.   I did not think I were so bold—and yet

I thy unmeek request will grant, and be
Thy humble, loyal, modest, mistress meek.

Victor. Nay, but my prattling, happy, gentle wife and queen.

Blanche That will I be if 'tis my father's wish.

Sly (*makes a low chuckle.*)

Blanche. What noise heard I?

Victor. Naught but the little rill. Come, dearest, come
with me.   (*Exeunt.*)

ACT II.

Scene 1. — *Summer-Land.* *A garden of Junior's.*
Gauntlet *at a little distance.* *Enter* Junior, *reading
a letter.*

Junior, (*not observing* Gauntlet, *reads aloud.*)
  "Methought it was an angel fair that slept.
  Silent I stood in rapturous wonder rapt.
  Then knowing that the sleeper wakens soon,
  I plucked a violet that nigh did bloom,
  And placed it in her hand, and quick did fly,
  Just as the sleeper, startled, oped her eye.
  For me, methought, she were the very bride,
  Seemingly free from every vice and pride."

Gauntlet (*aside.*) I will withdraw and overhear these words.

Junior. I will directly answer.

(Writes, and reads aloud.)

I counsel thee to first find who she is,
Seek her and find her parentage and name,
For she may be some foul fiend in disguise,
Who seeks to play a dangerous trick on thee.
And if she suit thee, win her to thy heart,
But win her first, before thou tell thy name,
For maidens oft refuse when they do find
Their lover is some one of high estate.
If thou wilt follow these my counsels, then
Wilt thou find good and prosperous success ;
And so, adieu. From Junior, thy dear friend,
Whose love for thee will never, never end.

(Exeunt.)

SCENE 2.—*In the Air.* GAUNTLET. *Enter* SLY.

Gauntlet. Ha! ha! my friend! and how dost do to-day?
Sly. Quite well! But dost thou know the bonny news?
Gauntlet. Nay! tell me quick, for I must soon be off.
Sly. Well, in good hunting-time the king, myself,

And all we hunters were within the wood,
When we did hear as sweet a song as e'er
Awoke the heavens to resound it well.

Gauntlet.　Proceed! Proceed!

Sly.　The king was raptured, and immediately
He left us and in search of it did go,
But soon returned, excited and well flushed,
As if some secret swelled within his breast;
And that day spake he incoherently,
And spent his time in pensive, lonesome mood.
The next day went we hunting in that wood,
We heard another song, and eagerly
He listened.　And when it did close, at once
Cautiously stepped he till far out of sight.
Said I, " I fain would know what this all means,"
And stepping cautiously, as did the king,
I saw a sight that made me chuckle, near,
A maiden, oh! so smiling and so fair!
That hid the sun behind a fleecy cloud:
And bending over her the king I saw,
And in his eyes I read the tale of love,
And I know it will not be long before
A maiden fair will be our king's sweet queen.

I quite forgot myself and laughed aloud.
She started, but the king did nothing hear.
Was I not glad when they did disappear!
Ha! ha! to think that no one knows but me!

Gauntlet. In one thing art thou mistaken.
I have a voice in this matter;
For I did overhear a letter read
By Junior, bosom friend of Victor, know,
Enough to make me curious, and so
I unobserved withdrew and overheard,
Which made me strangely to suspect the more,
Because he answered it, and read aloud.

Sly. Now for the fun of it, let's tell his sire,
For Victor would have told him long ago
If he'd a mind to. So let's him surprise
By getting his old father in a rage.

Gauntlet. But what if we be caught? Risk not too much.

Sly. Was I ever caught? Let us to Jerold. (*Exeunt.*)

SCENE 3.—*Fairy-Land. A room in the palace of Jerold.*
JEROLD. *Enter a* FAIRY.

Jerold. What is it thou dost want?

Fairy. My lord, there are two without who would speak
with thee.

14

Jerold.   Who are they?

Fairy.   Methinks one of them is Sly, the hunter. The other I know not.

Jerold.   Bring them hither.   (*Exit* FAIRY.)

I suspect something is not right.

           Enter SLY *and* GAUNTLET.

What dost want?

Gauntlet (*to Sly.*)   Speak thou first.

Sly.   Dost notice that the king doth favor hunting?

Jerold.   Aye, aye, proceed.

Sly.   The king hath found a new hunting-ground, and a new kind of game.

Jerold.   What dost thou mean?

Sly.   Cupid hath led thy son to the field of love, where he trieth his bow at a maiden whose name I know not. He'll not be long without a queen, my lord.

Jerold.   What maiden didst thou say?

Sly.   I know not. It seemeth 'twere best to question him. Who knows what the maiden might be? For all that she puts on a pleasing countenance, I like her not. Aye, my lord, I saw her consent to be his bride.

Jerold.   Without my knowledge and consent!

Sly. Aye, my lord.

Jerold. Right glad am I thou told me this. Hither, my trusty servant. (*Enter a fairy.*) Go thou and tell the king I would speak with him. (*Exit fairy.*) We shall soon see.

Enter VICTOR.

Victor. Good morrow, my father! All does not seem to be right.

Jerold. Good morrow! What hast been doing lately?

Victor. I have been boating, hunting, taking journeys to summer-land in the evening. In the day-time I work as do other fays, and in sleeping-time I sleep—

Rocked by the wind in the lily pale,

Lulled by the voice of the nightingale.

Jerold. Where hast been hunting?

Victor. In the woods, of course. By the way, dost know of the great accident that happened in the bee-hunter's garden?

Jerold. Nay, but tell me where hast been hunting?

Victor. In the woods, father. Did I not tell thee? But—

Jerold. What didst thou shoot?

Victor. Why, we were after humming birds; now I think of it—

Jerold. Nay; but tell what luck didst thou meet with?

Victor.   Splendid luck! we caught three apiece.

Jerold.   Dost recognize this fay? (SLY *comes forward.*)

Victor.   Aye, sir; he is one of my best hunters.

Jerold.   He declareth that he saw thee hunting a strange maiden in the field of love! Is that so? without my consent or knowledge?

Victor.   What, ho! how came this known?

Jerold.   But say, hast thou?

Victor.   Aye, my lord; I have captured as lovely a maiden as ever breathed!

Jerold.   Oh, thou rogue! Who may she be?

Victor.   Her name is Blanche. She is daughter to Count Hyacinth. Methinks thou knowest him.

Jerold.   What, he? I never had better friend than he! Bring her hither.

Victor.   Aye, that I will.   (*Exit* VICTOR.)

Jerold.   This land doth roll through many a wondrous course,

But stranger still life's ever changeful way.

(*Soft music.*)

Enter BLANCHE, VICTOR, *and* FAIRIES *attending.* BLANCHE *and* VICTOR *kneel to* JEROLD.

Jerold.   Look down, oh Jove! pronounce thy blessing on
    this pair,
And Hymen! waft the couple into one!
And Venus! in their hearts inspire
Love's ardent, joining, warm, sweet fire.
Cupid! he hath done his part,
For he hath fired his gilded dart
Into either's loving heart.

(FAIRIES *sing in chorus.*)

Song.

Queen, we sweetly welcome thee,
Loving subjects will we be,
Ever waiting at thy will,
None could better thy place fill.
We'll gather thee the sweetest flowers
That ever grew in fairy bowers.
We will waft thee as sweet and refreshing breeze
As ever played round the orange trees.
We will feed thee with honey, and tell thee many a
    tale,
Have thee sung to sleep by a nightingale.
We will dance for thee on the smooth bright green,
    14*

So welcome, welcome, welcome sweet queen.

Victor.   Now crown her with the fairest wreath

Of violets and baby's breath!

(She is crowned.   Exeunt.)

ACT III.

(Two or three hundred years after.)

Scene 1.—*Fairy-Land.   A room in the palace of* Victor.
Victor, Blanche, *and* Eva.

Victor (to Eva.)   Where doth thy work lie to-day, my pet ?

Eva.   To-day I sweep the cobwebs from the sky,

Those that the gloom-fays build from cloud to cloud,

To interfere with our most just exploits.

Blanche.   I fear to have thee go, I know not why ;

Adieu ! may nothing harm my Evening Star !

What is this strange, unwonted, half-felt fear ?

Why do I stay mine arms about thy neck ?

Some secret feeling prompts me so to do.

Let not, oh Jove ! these dark, proud, star-like eyes,

This queenly forehead, and these snow-white arms,

This heart, which proudly beats most royal blood,

Fade from my sight ! God keep my Evening Star !

Victor.   Thy fears are vain, for in a mother's breast
      Fears often reign when there no danger is.
Eva.   I must be gone.   Adieu! adieu! adieu!

      (Exit Eva.)

Blanche.   I'll shake this trouble off, foolish am I,
      What harm can reach my gentle Evening Star?
      Her smile would charm away the evil fiend,
      What creature ever dares to harm the pure?

      (Exeunt.)

Scene 2.—*In the air above Fairy-Land.   Above, the pleasure garden, royal palace, and Count's castle.   Enter* Eva, *returning from her work.*

Eva.   I fain would rest my weary self awhile,
      Pillowed upon some fleet-winged, secret cloud;
      For to the wearied soul there's nought like sleep.
      Then doth the mind on fleetest, softest wings
      Flee to the bright domain of dreamland; there
      To roam through most exquisite gardens fair,
      To taste delicious fruit, to rest in bowers
      Where grow most brilliant and most fragrant flowers.
      But I must go, for something prompts me on;
      Besides, a fear reigns in my mother's breast,

And I would not affright her in the least
More than I have by lingering for rest—
I am afeared I've e'en now stayed too long.

(*As she is about to go, horrible sounds. Enter* NIGHT-
SHADE.)

Nightshade.   What art doing here?   If thou tellest not
I'll crush thee like a worm to the ground.

Eva.   I went to sweep the cobwebs from the sky.

Nightshade.   That did I not forbid thee long ago?
Those cobwebs by incessant labor hard
Were built at last, by my hard working fays.
All only to be swept by evil hands!

Eva.   Your grace, I pardon beg.   I knew it not.

Nightshade.   Thy father knew it if didst not thyself.
It comes back on thee.   So I'll punish thee.
Thou'lt have no voice except the dashing sound
Of thy dark waves on the resounding shore.
Thy waves shall dance, but never, never more
Thy fleet foot on the smooth cut ring of green
Shall keep time to the nightingale's sweet voice!
No more! I'll soon have thee from off my hands.

(*Touches her with his wand.   A river flows from her mouth
into Fairy-Land.   Enter a Fairy at a distance,
observing them.*)

Fairy (*aside.*) What does this mean? She surely cannot be the king's daughter? As for the other, I
know him too well!

Eva. May God avenge the evil work which the treacher-
ous hath wrought upon the innocent!

(*As she sinks into the river, low moanings, hideous
noises, and mocking laughter are heard.   Exeunt.*)

SCENE 3.—*Fairy-Land.   A room in the palace of* VICTOR.
VICTOR *and* BLANCHE.

Blanche. My trouble more increases. Some time past
I felt a sudden shock come o'er my mind;
And I did seem to weep within myself.
Take warning, dearest, all cannot be right.

Victor. I thought thou wouldst forget it in thy work.

Blanche. Ah, no! it only clings to me the more.

Victor. Then 'tis a real feeling—though 'tis strange
That no such fear within my breast doth range.

Blanche. None but a mother knows a mother's fear.

Enter a FAIRY.

Fairy. My lord, there is one who wishes to speak with
thee.

Victor. Bring him directly.   (*Exit* FAIRY.)

Blanche.   My breast throbs quickly, and my breath comes
     thick,
    And now methinks some evidence we'll get.

Victor.   A little secret fear now seems to cross
    My troubled mind.   Dear wife, all is not right.
       Enter the FAY, *flushed and excited.*

Fay.   Sad news, my lord!

Victor.   Proceed, quickly!

Fay.   I busy roamed about the drowsy sky,
    Plucking the dew drops from the silver clouds,
    I saw your daughter, and old Nightshade by.
    A river flowed from out her firm blanched lips
    Into this land, and she sank in and drowned;
    And mocking laughter heard was all around,
    And hideous noises, and a moaning sound,
    And first I quickly came to tell you it.
                 (BLANCHE *swoons.*)
    Weep not, my lord, one for the best must hope.

Victor.   Oh! why should it be she!   She snatched away
    All in her lovely bloom of maidenhood!
    Oh bitter disappointment!   I had thought
    One day to place upon her head the crown!
    No maid in elf-land is as fair as she!

What fairy has such tranquil, lake-like eyes?
I oft at hearing her sweet voice was tricked,
Thinking her some sweet mavis singing gay!
But no! the mavis doth no sorrow know!
Ah! happy bird! I'd willingly exchange
My royal robes and crown for thy light heart!
Alas! alas! oh fate, thou'rt terrible!

(He weeps.)

Fairy.   Take it not so, my lord, 'tis for the best.
Thou art as weak at heart as thy fair wife.
For shame! look you where she doth swooning lie,
Whilst thou, who ought'st to keep thy courage up
Dost show a nature cowardly and weak,
Which sets a bad example to thy fays.
Thou, who shouldst be most strong, art faltering.
Cheer up, and strengthen yet thy courage well!

Victor.   I thank thee, noble fay, for thy brave hint,
I am ashamed; I'll get my courage up.
But oh? it came so sudden. 'Twas a shock
That drove me from my senses, and made me
As weak and faltering as womankind.
(*To attendants.*)   Bear her away, and attend her in
her swoon.   (*Exeunt.*)

SCENE 4.—*The same. In the House of Representatives.*
VICTOR, BLANCHE, *and all the* FAYS *of Fairy-Land.*

Victor (rises and reads.)

Public Act of the Fairy-Land Congress :

Owing to the turning of my daughter Eva into a river
by Nightshade, present king of Gloom-land, and for
various past injuries done by him, I, Victor, present
king of Fairy-Land, do now, before my kingdom,
solemnly declare war against the above-named Nightshade.

All.   Hurrah ! hurrah !

Victor.   And now, brethren, as our force is small, I move
that we request Summer-Land to join with us.

All.   Agreed.

Victor.   And let us fight our noblest, bravest fight,
And trample down the foe with scornful foot.
Long may the dauntless yellow, black and blue
Wave o'er the warriors brave of Fairy-Land !
We'll be the dauntless dandelions brave,
Which, after being trampled under foot
Spring up again as daring as before.
We'll bring our evil foe to very shame,

And he that once did laugh at us with scorn
Shall kneel and beg for mercy at our feet!

All.   Hurrah! hurrah! Long may the yellow, black,
and blue, wave above Elf-Land! Long live King
Victor! Long live Queen Blanche! Long let the
crown sparkle upon their brows! Hurrah! hurrah!

Victor.   God lead us!   (*Exeunt.*)

ACT IV.

Scene 1.—*Summer-Land.   In the palace of* Genu.
Genu *and all the* Sylphids *of Summer-Land.*

Genu (rising.)   I have received a letter from Fairy-Land
informing me that Victor hath declared war against
Gloom-Land, being very wrathful at Nightshade for
the changing of his daughter into a river. As their
force is small, they request us to aid them with a small
army. Now what shall we do? Shall we let them
fight and weep, while we lie comfortably enjoying
ourselves?

Sylphids.   No! no! we will shed our blood for the rights
of Fairy-Land.

Genu.   That is right. We will not be cowardly. Let us
15

gather together five millions of brave Sylphids. I
will go myself.

Sylphids. Nay! double the five millions.

Genu. My noble people! I am proud of you! Let us
nobly tread upon the enemies of Fairy-Land.

Sylphids. Aye! aye! Hurrah! hurrah! hurrah!

(*Exeunt.*)

Scene 2.—*In the Air. War music. Enter at opposite
doors the armies of Summer-Land and Fairy-Land, com-
manded by* Victor *and* Genu.

Victor. Noble Genu! We thank thee fervently for this.
We feel that we need thee, though we have no claims.

Genu. It is just. Dost thou think us so cowardly as to
sit idly lolling around, whilst thou dost struggle on the
battle-field? Nay! we hope not!

(*Horrible music heard from without.*)

Hark! the enemy is approaching.   (*Exeunt.*)

Scene 3.—*Gloom-Land. On a plain. Enter a* Gloomfairy *and a* Soldier *of Gloom-Land.*

Gloomfairy. How goes the war?

Soldier. Poorly. Fairy-Land has the upper hand. What
think you? Summer-Land hath joined it!

Gloomfay. Dost thou speak truth?

Soldier. Aye, as I stand here. There's scarce hope for us.

Gloomfay. How many went to battle?

Soldier. Fifteen millions.

Gloomfay. And are they not able to win?

Soldier. A sort of stupid sleepiness seems to have come over us.

Gloomfay. Think you the country is in danger?

Soldier. Well, in sooth, I know not. But if his highness should do something extra, we should fare better.

(Horns sound.)

Hark! I must be gone. (Exeunt.)

SCENE 4.—*Before the tent of* NIGHTSHADE. *Enter* NIGHTSHADE *and a* SOLDIER *of Gloomland.*

Nightshade. How goes the war?

Soldier. Worse and worse, my lord.

Nightshade. Go, thou, fetch me the black flower of the phymarda, that grows by the side of yon hill, whose power can change the form into any shape the user chooseth, provided it be inflicted on another person. (*Exit Soldier.*) Ha! ha! ha! Thou needst not say, "worse and worse." Thou mayst freely say, "better and better." Fairies always were such un-suspecting creatures. Fairy-Land and Summer-Land shall be mine before long. Fairy-Land shall be mine before the day is out. And as for Summer-Land—why the Sylphids are too lazy to fight much. Ha! ha! They will both be mine soon. Ha! ha! ha! ha! ha!

(*Re-enter* SOLDIER *with a black flower.*)

Aye, there it is. Give it me quickly. (*Exeunt.*)

ACT V.

SCENE 1.—*Fairy-Land. In the palace of* VICTOR.
BLANCHE *and* ATTENDANTS.

Blanche. Alas, he comes not! It is past the hour since he did promise. Oh! the bloody war, that calls the husbands from their weeping wives! I fear that all not right is, or he'd come.

Attendant. Cheer up, my lady. Look! he cometh now!

(*Enter* VICTOR, *singing.*)

Victor. Oh! where can be my loving wife?
Cheer up, my joy, my light, my life!
Cheer up my Blanche! good news I'm bringing,
The battle Fairy-Land is winning!

Blanche. Ah! I thought thou wouldst never come!

(They embrace each other.)

     The days were long without thee,
      The days were sad and drear,
     From worrying about thee
      And wishing thou wert here.

Victor. I have some business, dearest, to attend to, but will soon be back.   (*Exit.*)

Blanche (*to attendant.*) Away with thee, and let me muse.

Attendant. We fear that harm may reach thee with his long and powerful arms, from which none can escape.

Blanche. I feel no danger. Away! away!

(Exeunt ATTENDANTS.)

Now I can weep, unheard and undisturbed.

(Horrible sounds.)

Enter NIGHTSHADE.

Nightshade. Come with me! I'll take care of you.

Blanche. I pray you!

Nightshade. No loitering. Here, bear her away.

(*Enter* GLOOMFAYS, *who bear her away. Ha! ha! ha! ha! ha! Exit leaving a stake in the floor with a sentence around it. In a few moments re-enter* VICTOR.)

Victor. What, gone! I should have thought thou

wouldst have stayed for me! What means this stake?
(*Reads*—"*Nightshade hath Blanche safe!*") Oh!
woe! Why stayed I not with her? I will directly
and tell Jerold.   (*Exit.*)

SCENE 2.—*Fairy-Land. In the palace of* JEROLD.
Enter VICTOR.

Victor. Hither, my father, directly. Where art?
                (*Enter a little yellow dog.*)
What meaneth this? I called my father, not a dog.
But here is a collar with letters on it. (*Reads*—"*I
am thy father.*")

What does this mean? Alas I do but dream!
Dreamland, release me from thy cruel bonds.
Dreams once were pleasant, now they're mean to me.
I will to Herold's and tell what I've seen.

                        (*Exit.*)

SCENE 3.—*Fairy-Land. In front of* VICTOR'S *palace,
near the steps. Ugly sounds. Enter* NIGHTSHADE *with
the phymarda.*

Nightshade. And now I'll end my work successfully,
    And he who at this hour calls him king,
    Shall humbled be into a little child—
    And all my fays shall laugh him unto scorn.

(He smears the steps with the flower, and dances around them to hideous sounds, laughter, and moans. Exit NIGHTSHADE *laughing. Enter* VICTOR.

Victor. I've traveled round from palace unto hall,
But all have changed. Among my subjects dear
There is not one who has not changed his shape
Into some beastly form—some cat or dog,
Some cow, some calf, some chicken, or some horse!
What will become of us? I fain would die!
What more have I to care for in this land?
My wife is stolen, and my subjects changed!
Alas! I've nought to care for but myself.
Oh! for my happy, unsuspecting youth!
Alas! how proudly won I my fair Blanche!
How gaily danced I on the rings of green!
Alas! those happy days are passed for me!
Cold Sorrow! I'll abide upon thy breast!

(As he goes up the steps his kingly garments fall from him, and he becomes a human being. Exeunt.)